# CLEARLY
## COMMUNICATING
# CHRIST

# CLEARLY COMMUNICATING CHRIST

*Breaking
Down Barriers
to Effective
Communication*

# LANDA COPE

**PUBLISHING**

*A Ministry Of Youth With A Mission*

P.O. Box 55787, Seattle, WA 98155

YWAM Publishing is the publishing ministry of Youth With A Mission. Youth With A Mission (YWAM) is an international missionary organization of Christians from many denominations dedicated to presenting Jesus Christ to this generation. To this end, YWAM has focused it's efforts in three main areas: 1) Training and equipping believers for their part in fulfilling the Great Commission (Matthew 28:19). 2) Personal evangelism. 3) Mercy ministry (medical and relief work).

For a free catalog of books and materials write or call:

YWAM Publishing

P.O. Box 55787, Seattle, WA 98155

(206)771-1153 or (800) 922-2143

*To Don and Deyon, who gave me the chance to learn God's ways in communication.*
*To Loren, who gave me the platform to teach.*
*And to Darlene, who gave me the courage.*

# Acknowledgments

I suppose every writer coming to the acknowledgment page for the first time feels the need to thank the whole world. Who in my life has not been a part of this project in some way? What an impossible task! But here are my humble offerings.

I have to begin with Dad, who taught me that "a job worth doing is worth doing well," and Mom, who taught me to ask good questions. Then there are my three siblings, who never tolerated shallow arguments.

There are the host of helpers—Jenny, Jill, Nancy, LaPrelle, Dennis—who typed, advised, and organized. Rick, who got me jump-started on the first draft. Craig and Fiona, who helped me bring in the final one. And I must not forget Jim, Pam, and Warren of YWAM Publishing.

Dr. Doug Feaver, Dr. Mel Hanna, Dr. Bill Brown, and Dr. Jim Engel all deserve special mention for helping pilot the research. Dr. Charles Davis helped with last-minute scrutiny. And Judith Cespedes, without whom this project may never have been finished, and who did all the footnoting and backup research.

My college staff, especially John and Jean, deserve

great thanks for releasing me all those days from the office. And John and Barbara for the straight talk that got the job done.

Finally, thanks to John and Elizabeth Sherrill, who shared a kindred spirit in the middle of a long tunnel, and to Janice Rogers, who turned the unreadable around.

# Table of Contents

# Foreword

CHRISTIANS ARE SO FAMILIAR with the words of St. Paul, "I have become all things to all men, so that by all possible means I might save some" (I Corinthians 9:22) that the amazingly radical nature of the statement often simply passes them by.

The principle seems clear enough: For the Gospel to take root among any people, in any class, in any nation of the world, it must be conveyed in a manner that is *totally* integrated into the culture of the group to which it is being preached. Less obvious is the fact that the mimicking of a language, or even an accent within a language, is not enough.

Just as the Son of God chose to identify in both biological and genealogical ways with the Jews to whom He was sent, so the Gospel must resonate at levels of human response so deep and so intuitive that the receiving group welcomes the message almost like a long-lost cousin.

How is that done?

Hundreds of square miles of forest have been cut down to publish the books over the centuries that have attempted to answer this question. The challenging irony of our own day is that though world is now more than ever truly one in terms of communication links between its various parts, a counter-trend of increased local tribalism seems to be just as strong. More than ever before, separate ethnic, economic, or religious groups demand that any message spoken to them be delivered in their own particular private *lingua*. It is not so much "political correctness" here as what might be termed "identity correctness": Does the message-delivering person *really* know who or what we are and what is important to us?

Thus—to take an example at random, but one touched upon in this book—to preach to Dutch bikers and druggies in Amsterdam, it is clearly not sufficient merely to know Dutch fluently. The evangelist to this group needs both to understand and to *empathize with* at a very deep level the particular social and philosophical universe from which this sub-culture derives. The issue, moreover, is not just "cross-cultural evangelism," the earnest staple of many missionary schools and Christian seminaries. It is understanding the very heart of Jesus Christ Himself in His own reaching out to the lost sheep of first-century Palestine.

Landa Cope has brilliantly and succinctly distilled the insights and experience from decades of her own forays into evangelism into more countries and regions of the world than most Christians are capable even of naming. Ranging from Amsterdam to Bangkok with illustrations of both her successes and her candidly admitted failures, she etches out the fundamental keys to shaping an evangelism that honors both its audience and the One who commissioned it. There are no formulae here, no three easy steps (or three easy anything), no references to this or that textbook of the correct way: just sharp insights into how the Lord dealt with challenges which were in His own context quite as daunting as any that face modern missionaries.

Landa Cope's area of specialty in the Christian academic environment (at various campuses of the University of the Nations, Kailua-Kona, Hawaii) has been communications. At its core, indeed, this book is about communicating. But it is more importantly a reflection of a preoccupation resting much deeper within Landa's own heart, namely *evangelism.* Every evangelical Christian, if he or she is serious about the Christian walk, must wrestle with this notion sooner or later. By reading Landa Cope's well-written and fascinating book, that wrestling is certain to be not just a challenge, but a source of excitement.

David Aikman
Burke, Virginia

# Introduction

IT WAS A COLD, WET South Island morning, and everything in my weary body said, "Roll over. You need the sleep." But I remembered that this might be my only chance to watch from on board as our vessel pulled out of a New Zealand port.

I stumbled out of my bunk, threw on some clothes, grabbed a mug of coffee, and headed up three decks to the bridge. No one was there, which was fine with me. Months of frantic media work before and after each of our 18 ports of call in New Zealand had left me physically depleted and emotionally dangerous. I should have worn a sign that said, "You do not want to talk to this woman. It's not worth the risk." I huddled inside my jacket, clutching my coffee, as our crew cast off.

Ships are the largest moving objects on earth, and their movement near land is nearly imperceptible. It has a strange, slow-motion majesty. That morning, as we eased from the dock, people began to arrive in cars and wave at the ship. *That's nice,* I thought, turning my back to the wind. The exit from this particular port was a channel that ran along the main road of town.

As we crept along the channel, more and more cars

began to stop on the street. I leaned on the rail and watched. Now all the cars were stopped on this busy thoroughfare. People were jumping out and waving their arms, their sweaters, and their jackets. These were not just friends of the ship, but everyone traveling down that street that morning. Their enthusiasm and joy drifted over the cold channel waters and ignited my soul.

Suddenly the Spirit of the Lord opened my eyes and I began to realize what I was seeing. A whole town, a community of people—Christians and non-Christians—were waving...at a ship? No, a mere hunk of metal couldn't elicit that much enthusiasm. At what, then? What had generated this spontaneous and contagious joy? It was the Lord. As they waved at the ship, they were worshiping. Whether they knew God in a personal way, they had been touched by something so wonderful, they knew they had to respond. "Every knee shall bow, every tongue confess that Jesus Christ is Lord." ...The song played over and over in my mind.

From the beginning God had told us as a mission that He would use us to disciple nations. I believed it, but until that morning leaving New Zealand, I had thought this would be many decades in the future, when we were old and much wiser.

Our six-month, 18-port visit to New Zealand had generated 99% national awareness of the ship ministry, and had exposed many thousands to God's merciful heart for the suffering. The New Zealanders gave so much aid for hurricane-devastated Fiji that we had enough to fill our cargo holds twice, necessitating a return voyage. One hundred fifty thousand people visited the ship and heard a measure of the Gospel. Even more attended land-based functions and evangelistic events. Only the Lord knows how many came to know Him during that time period. Youth With A Mission had to start schools all over the country to try to meet the desire for missions training. During the next year, every Bible school in the country was filled to capacity.

All of this came from one small, short-term missions tour. During our time there, God also gave us principles of how to share our vision with non-Christian radio, television, and print media. Reporters covered the story in city newspapers in every port and often nationally during our stay. They were touched by the truth, they reported the truth, and God was glorified throughout the nation.

I began to see what God had taught us, and I wanted to share it with others. What if every ministry in every nation had these same principles of communication God had taught us?

The College of Communication for the University of the Nations was born in my heart that morning on the bridge. I would never again expect so little. I saw what truth communicated with the wisdom of God could accomplish. I knew then that I would soon leave the ship, even though it had been the most exciting and fulfilling ministry opportunity of my life. I would leave because God needed an army—an army of anointed, skilled communicators in every nation of the world to lift the name of Jesus.

The principles in this book are those that God taught me, not only on the ship, but in ten hectic years of developing and implementing communication strategies on four continents. I have applied these principles in many varied and complicated communications challenges, including my own life. They work. They will work for you. They will work in your marriage, with your children, your loved ones, your fellowships, and especially in your efforts to reach the lost. These principles will work for any message with any audience, because they are God's principles of communication.

My prayer for you as you read this book is that your heart and mind will explode as the Holy Spirit reveals truth, and that you will be permanently altered in your concept of how to get your message across....to the Glory of God.

Landa Lea Cope
Riggins, Idaho

# Part I

## Why We Can Communicate

*"Moses said to the Lord, 'I am slow of speech and tongue.' The Lord said to him, 'Who gave man his mouth?...Is it not I, the Lord? Now go; I will help you speak and will teach you what to say.'"*
*(Exodus 4:10-12)*

# Chapter One

✎

# *You Can Communicate!*

✎

*"A word aptly spoken is like apples of gold
in settings of silver" (Proverbs 25:11).*

I HAVE ALWAYS DISLIKED the cold approach of street witnessing. But I was in Venice as part of an evangelism effort, and was determined to make the best of it.

We spilled out of the host church and made our way to the streets and piazzas of this grand city. My eyes searched the flow of humanity passing in the sunshine. Surely there was someone I should speak to...someone who at least understood English.

Then I spotted her: a quiet, artsy-looking young woman sitting alone on a bench beside the avenue. I went over and asked if she spoke English.

"Ay leetle," she said in her thick Italian accent. That was all I needed. I sat beside her and the floodgates opened. For the next 30 to 45 minutes I gave this young lady a most glorious presentation of the Bible, from Genesis to Revelation. I barely paused for breath. She was patient and didn't interrupt, even nodding at various appropriate points.

I finished and smiled at her, signaling her opportunity to respond. She sat there quietly, looking intent. Finally, holding her hands in front of her as if patting an invisible shield, she said, "Yu...Yu like...breeck wall!"

I was devastated! Here I was, the Great Evangelical Talking Machine, giving my spiel. I hadn't shown any interest in who she was, where she was coming from, or what her interests were. I was there to reel off my message, register her decision, and move on. And she had nailed me. That was exactly what I was, a brick wall. I had a lot to learn about communicating the Gospel.

I don't feel I'm unique in my struggle to communicate effectively. The Body of Christ around the world wrestles with Jesus' command to preach the Gospel to every creature. Yet in the face of staggering need—like 3.58 billion who have never once heard of Jesus,[1] more than 11,000 people groups with no Gospel witness,[2] and huge barriers separating us (such as the hostility of Islamic cultures and the cool indifference of post-Christian Europe)—we can feel a bit overwhelmed.

Evangelism isn't the only communication challenge we face, either. Parents and children, husbands and wives, friends, young men and women who have fallen in love, extended family members, social workers, civic servants, employers and employees, and members of congregations...virtually anyone who cares about people has had difficulty communicating.

At the heart of most human problems lies a problem with communication. For instance, a study found that in 77% of all divorces in the United States, lack of communication was the major factor.[3]

The assistant chief of police in a large city once told me of the frustration his men and women face on the streets of the inner city. A cauldron of races, cultures, and languages have created a world where the Anglo-Saxon cop is a stranger. It's a dangerous world, where words, emotions, and even gestures can be misunderstood in a split second, leading to violence and death.

## Seeing Things Differently

The ad for an electric company in a magazine said, "You can't do things differently until you see things differently."

If we struggle to communicate, we need to see the process differently. We need a perspective that will help us solve the daily myriad of communication problems we face. And God is ready and willing to give us that new perspective. He wants to turn our heads around and give us much greater understanding. He wants to give us confidence that we can reach the one who is closest to us, as well as every creature (Mark 16:15).

## Getting Rid of Old Ideas

Christians often envy the communication industry. We wish we could make movies like "they" do, movies with impact. We wish we could write books like "they" do, with million-dollar sales. We look at television and say, "If we could just have Christian television programs that influence so many!"

As we envy the skill of the world, we begin to think that the answer is to model ourselves after them. If we could mimic what they have done, we could communicate the Christian message more effectively. We base this idea on the premise that "they" are doing a good job. But are they? Does the world understand communication?

Let's look at some statistics from just one arena of communication: advertising in the print media. Let's say you buy a one-page, four-color ad in *Time* magazine for $147,000 to advertise your new invention: "Global Statistics Software—All the national statistics of the world on one optic disc." The cost of the ad is based on the number of people who will receive it. In this case the circulation is 4.3 million weekly. In addition to the cost of the ad, you also pay for the copy, design, and art work—say, $2,000 to $5,000. It's the best print ad you have ever produced for your company, GlobeStat, Inc.

What can you expect as a return on your hard-earned $150,000 investment? Here's what research shows:

Forty-four percent of the people who flip through the magazine will notice your ad. Thirty-five percent will read enough to identify your brand. Nine percent will read most of your copy.[4]

Are these the results you expected? How would you feel if I said that nine percent of all the people you ever communicate with will know what you said? Why do advertisers spend the money? Because nine percent of

4.3 million is 387,000—a lot of people thinking about GlobeStat, Inc. Three percent could actually buy your software. As long as the profit margin is there, the investment is worth it.

And what about that giant of communication, television? In *TV Guide*, American humorist Steve Allen called television "junk food for the mind." Most will agree that much television programming is silly. Only in television ads do viewers jump up and down with excitement over new shows. Most of the laughter is canned, and most of the dramas follow predictable formulas. How many shows can you remember 48 hours or a week later?

Then why do people watch television? Primarily because there is nothing better to do. I've read that the fluctuating colors and patterns on the screen have the same effect of raising the alpha waves in the brain as a fireplace does, producing relaxation. You could get the same benefit by merely watching the test pattern after a television station signs off! Television offers relaxation and live coverage of the occasional breaking news event, but it hardly qualifies as great communication.

How many great movies or books have you seen or read? How many can you remember a month later? On a scale of 1 to 10, how many would you rate as a 10? I see movies that the critics praise, I read books that receive great reviews. But as time passes, I remember little of their content. Occasionally I'm halfway through a book before realizing I've already read it! Much of what I see is only average, and some isn't even that good. Often a big movie studio pours more than $100 million into a box-office dud, and a noted author produces a book guaranteed to put anyone to sleep.

There is a big difference between mass communication and effective communication. This "Communication Age" is more like the "Proliferation of Information Age"—a lot of noise is filling the silence of the planet. Even when we have 500 channels on television, will we be able to find anything worth watching? The world's communication giants are not necessarily communicating. They are not necessarily getting their message through to anyone.

## Is the Church Communicating?

Perhaps we need to see our own lack of effective communication more clearly. Does the Bible say, "Go into all the world and preach the Gospel to nine percent?" Are you going to be satisfied with a three-percent response rate to the Gospel?

You and I and the entire Body of Christ have been charged with the responsibility of reaching the whole world. That's a huge goal. More personally, each one of us wants to see Christ lived out in every relationship of our life. Each one of us wants to reach our world. But to do that, we need help, and the best teacher is God Himself.

## God Has the Answers.

Why learn God's method of communication? Not because we have an emotional obligation to God, but because He is the master of communication, and His methods work. We don't have to slavishly imitate the world's communication, putting a thin Christian veneer over it. We can learn God's communication principles, try them, measure them, and see the results. We can be better communicators in every area of our lives.

So let's do it! Let's stop envying the world, put our noses into the Word of God, and get His perspective.

# Chapter Two

ꟾꟾ

# *God and Communication*

ꟾꟾ

*"In the beginning was the Word, and the Word
was with God, and the Word was God".
(John 1:1).*

A WELL-KNOWN PASTOR invited a visiting preacher to his home for dinner. The pastor's children, including his three-year-old son, were gathered around the beautifully set table. They clasped hands and bowed their heads for the blessing.

The pastor said a dignified grace fitting the formality of the occasion, closing with, "And in the name of Jesus we pray, Amen." The others reverently echoed, "Amen."

Suddenly, in a piercing voice, the three-year-old blurted: "Jesus, Jesus, Jesus! That's all we hear around here, and He don't say nothin'."

We may smile, but there are lots of people who would echo the sentiments of that three-year-old. Some have gone so far as to build their theology around the concept of a "silent" or a "lonely" God. But this isn't the God of the Bible. As Francis Schaeffer said in the title of his book, *He Is There and He Is Not Silent.*

## God *Is* Communication.

The book of John begins with, "In the beginning was the Word, and the Word was God." A.W. Tozer said, "An intelligent, plain man, untaught in the truths of Christianity...would likely conclude that John meant to teach that it is the nature of God to speak, to communicate His thoughts to others. And he would be right."[5] God is so synonymous with communication that Scripture refers to Him as the Word, the Logos of Life.

It is just as impossible to separate the God of the Bible from the concept of communication as it is to separate Him from the concept of love. God is love. And God is communication.

Communication existed before the creation of the human race. According to the Bible, it did not come into being with the forming of Adam, but existed before him. God has always related interpersonally within the Trinity: the Father, the Son, and the Holy Spirit. Members of the Trinity speak to one another (Genesis 1:26). The Bible also shows brief glimpses of other communication inside heaven. Music is used in continual worship, with lyrics being sung before God's throne (Revelation 15:3). We hear about the book of life in heaven (Revelation 21:27). In Job 1:6, we see God dialoguing with Lucifer.

## Spiritual Communication

We know there is communication going on in heaven, but that does not mean it is speech as we know it. Very likely the members of the Trinity can communicate in other ways. This spiritual communication has no beginning, as God has no beginning. Speech is a relatively new method of communication compared to spiritual communication. And this most powerful form of communication knows no limits. God is a spiritual being, and can communicate anywhere, at will (Psalm 139). We marvel at satellite communication, giving nearly instant access to information over long distances. But this is a slow, creaky system compared to God's communication capabilities.

## God Is Committed to Communication.

The God of the Bible is passionately committed to communication. He's not aloof, but sacrificially seeks to rebuild relationship bridges which have been torn down. We would be in trouble if this were not so, because He sought us when we were running from Him (I John 4:19; Romans 5:8-10). He's committed to communication.

When God created human beings, male and female, He walked and talked with them in the Garden on a daily basis. When the Fall separated our race from God, God committed Himself unto death to see us restored. He sent His prophets with His words. He inspired others to write His Word down. He supernaturally wrote His own words on the tablets given to Moses at Mount Sinai, and on the wall of King Belshazzar's palace. He sent His own Son to personally embody and bear His message.

Why all this commitment? John 3:16 makes it clear. Because He loves us. And love longs to communicate.

## God Communicates Effectively With Every Human Being.

When I was a small child, I remember lying in the grass on warm summer nights, looking at the starlit skies and wishing I could find the book that told me everything about everything. Little did I know I was lying there looking up at some of God's most eloquent communication.

Romans 1:20 makes this incredible statement: "For since the creation of the world God's invisible qualities—his eternal power and divine nature—have been clearly seen, being understood from what has been made, so that men are without excuse."

What this means is that you can look at the creation and see qualities of God's character. You can see His power: The 1980 eruption of Mt. St. Helens in Washington State was estimated to be 500 times as powerful as the atomic bomb dropped on Hiroshima. You can see His faithfulness: The seasons never fail, and the sun rises predictably every morning. You can see the mercy of God: It rains on the atheist's farm as well as on the Christian's farm.

Every science proves God is orderly. Whether we zoom in with microscopes to the most infinitesimal unit or use the most powerful telescopes to probe the farthest reaches of the universe, everything we find is ordered. The universe is God's communication of Himself, and God is orderly.

Whatever scientific truth is discovered is truth about Him. When a physicist discovers a new law, He is finding a truth that God has written about Himself.

## We Don't Want to Hear.

If all humanity receives God's communication, why don't we all acknowledge the truth? Because we don't want to. The problem between man and God is not that He is not communicating, or that He is communicating ineffectively. The problem is, not everyone wants to admit the possibility that He may exist.

Before I became a disciple of the Lord Jesus, I was an atheist for a time. I abandoned that belief when I realized an atheist must take a "blind leap of faith." It is impossible to prove a negative, philosophically or intellectually. No one can prove that God does not exist.

In his bestseller, *The Road Less Traveled*, Dr. Scott Peck came to the conclusion that God has to exist. As a psychiatrist, Peck said our greatest fear is that God does exist, and that He might want us to be like Him.[6]

At the writing of that book, Peck was not yet a believer in Christ, but a short while later, his honesty led him to Jesus.

The Bible shows us a picture of God's heart in communication. Throughout the book of Hosea, the Lord says (after trying unsuccessfully to reach the children of Israel): "I tried this and you wouldn't listen to Me, so I tried that. You still wouldn't listen to Me. I tried another tactic, and when that didn't work, I wept and agonized and tried something else" (my paraphrase).

In later chapters, we will see a fuller picture of how

God invested man with such power over his own destiny. For now, let's say that no barrier is too great for God's communication. But once we've communicated, decisions are still the domain of the individual (Deuteronomy 29:19-20; Joshua 24:15-18; I Kings 18:21).

## The Intimacy We Shrink From

Jesus says in a wonderful passage of John, "I no longer call you servants, because a servant does not know his master's business. Instead, I have called you friends, for everything that I learned from my Father I have made known to you" (John 15:15). Jesus indicates that one of the marks of friendship is open communication, and He seeks that kind of relationship with us. Jesus does not want mere servants, telling us what to do with no explanation. He wants friends.

However, we often prefer being God's servants to being His friends, because servanthood demands a much lower level of commitment and intimacy. A servant can be distant emotionally. Intimacy is intimidating by its very nature.

If you've never been intimidated by God, you've probably never experienced intimacy with Him. If He has never cut too close for comfort, you've probably not interacted with Him at the level He desires. Jesus offers open, unguarded communication as His standard of friendship.

## Pray Without Ceasing.

God desires communication in return, calling on us to "pray without ceasing" (I Thessalonians 5:17 NASB).

Does this sound impossible? Is your gut reaction, "What an enormous effort"? It *would* be impossible without intimacy.

When two people are in love and intimate with each other, they are constantly aware of one another. They know what is important to each other. They may even know how the other one is feeling. If separated for awhile, they can imagine what the other person is doing. There is an emotional and spiritual bond. Even if one is very busy and preoccupied, he or she is still aware that he or she is part of the other.

God wants that kind of intimacy with us. Whatever we are doing, wherever we are, He wants that emotional, spiritual link to bring a constant flow of communication.

We cannot separate the God of the Bible from communication. It is part of who He is, just as love is part of who He is. That is why He made us the way He did.

# Chapter Three

⚬⚬⚬

# *The Way We Are*

⚬⚬⚬

*"Now the Lord God had formed out of the
ground all the beasts of the field and all the birds
of the air. He brought them to the man to see
what he would name them; and whatever the
man called each living creature, that was its
name. So the man gave names to...all the
beasts of the field" (Genesis 2:19-20).*

GOD CREATED US for relationship. As
one writer said, "...All humans are bonding beings....Their yearning for intimacy is an internal magnet
which draws them, often unwittingly, toward God, for
whose intimate relationship they are created."[7] This is
very clear when we read the story of our origins in
Genesis.

Every afternoon God walked with the man and his wife, sharing with them the fellowship He continually experienced in His triune Being. Nothing compelled God to create or pursue humanity. It came out of His heart of love. And it still does.

Because love and intimacy only come through communication, communication is entwined in the story of the Garden of Eden. It shows that our first task as humans, our first expressed need, our first temptation, our first error, and finally, our first sin, all revolved around communication.

## The First Job: Creating Language

Adam was in the newly created Garden when God gave him his first real job. Imagine: Here was this fantastic new creation with wonderful abilities, and what was his first chance to apply some of them? A communications job! Adam began his work on earth by creating a language, putting together symbols of communication.

God could have named all the animals Himself, telling Adam what to call each one. But He gave that responsibility to Adam, agreeing to use the words man created. He said, "All right, Adam, if you want to call that an *elephant*, I'll call it an *elephant*."

This has been going on ever since. I have traveled to more than 70 countries, and wherever I go, I find that no matter what language the people speak, they hear from God in their own language.

We are still doing the same job Adam was given to do: creating new words to communicate to the world in which we live. When I was young, you were "neat" if others liked you. Later you were "cool," then "bad," then "awesome," then "rad," then "stupid-fresh." They will create more new words before this book can go to press.

We're still creating language. And God is moving right along with us, keeping up to date with our terms. Unlike frustrated parents or teachers, He is always current.

God made us for this task of communicating. It is our most ancient and significant skill. Not only are we able to do it, we were created to do it. It is one of our primary purposes.

## The First Problem: Loneliness

There were problems in paradise. It was a perfect place, a perfect time, and Adam had daily communication with God. Yet something was missing. The first of our species experienced loneliness. Adam, alone, was incomplete. He lacked that aspect of God's image some Bible scholars call "partnership."[8] God then completed His image in humans: He created woman along with man. Together, male and female, they could complete God's earthly picture of Himself.

"Partnership," that part of God's image expressed in the Trinity, could now be expressed by His creatures. They could fulfill their destiny, multiplying the reflections of His image and of their own image. Loneliness was resolved for Adam and for future generations. The wonderful communication and oneness known in the Godhead throughout eternity could now be experienced by the creatures among themselves.

It is important to note that the term *Adam* was

inclusively male and female. The Hebrew name "Adam," (*adham*), is generic and collective, such as the word *mankind*.[9] Genesis 5:1-2 emphasizes this plurality. "When God created man, he made him in the likeness of God. He created them male and female;...he blessed them and called them 'man' [*adham*]."

It's very interesting that no other name was used for the unified duo until after the Fall. After relationship was broken, Adam sought to differentiate himself from his partner by giving her a name separate from his own—Eve.[10]

## The First Temptation: To Doubt
## Our Capacity to Hear and Understand God

In Genesis chapter 3, we are given a glimpse of the origins of temptation. In the form of a snake, Lucifer entered the Garden and spoke to the woman. His first words show his manipulative strategy: "Did God really say...?"

Satan was too subtle to immediately challenge the truth of what God had said. Instead he stabbed a more vulnerable spot—Eve's confidence in her ability to hear God. Lucifer began his destruction by sowing seeds of doubt in the communication process between God and humanity.

I am amazed that this is still such a basic temptation to us. I have the opportunity of working with thousands of committed Christians from all over the world, and the doubt they express most often to me is in their ability to hear God. Obedience is not even a question: They will obey. But time and time again they are plagued by nagging questions of, "Is that really You, God?"

Satan's first attempt failed. The woman clarified exactly what God had said. So Satan lunged again with a flat denial of God's words. "You will not surely die..." or in other words, "That's what He *said*, but you don't understand what God *meant.*"

When the enemy cannot destroy our confidence in hearing God, his back-up strategy is to attack our confidence in being able to understand. Who are we to know what the Creator of the whole universe is trying to say?

The effective twist in this approach is that it puts all the emphasis on our ability to hear and understand rather than on God's ability to communicate with us clearly. We are looking at ourselves rather than at God, and that is always a mistake.

## The First Sin: Not Communicating

The one obvious solution to the great temptation to doubt God's Word was to ask God. But neither the man nor the woman thought of asking God to clarify His communication. They could have waited to ask Him when He walked with them every evening in the Garden. They had the source of all truth accessible to them on a daily basis. Why didn't they say, "Well, Mr. Snake, you have a thought there. Hold on till we talk to God, and we'll get back to you"? It would have been so simple, so reasonable.

If the first temptation was a result of the enemy sowing seeds of doubt about the reliability of what God spoke to man, then the first sin was discarding what God said and believing what His enemy said instead. The first sin was the result of a lack of open communication—going back to God and asking what He meant. Adam and Eve did not communicate with God; instead, they broke His law by eating the forbidden fruit.

## The First Mark of Sin:
## Breakdown of Communication

The deed was done! God's law had been broken, and within the seconds it took to disobey, the human race was transformed permanently and irrevocably from God's nature to a sinful nature. Nothing would restore that fallen condition until Christ died on the cross.

What did sin look like in those first few moments? Close your eyes and try to imagine it. It was milliseconds after the fruit was eaten. Do you see lying? Gossip and backbiting? Cheating? Stealing? Do you see adults taking illegal drugs to escape life's pain, and then handing them to children? Do you see war's bloody violence against men, women, and children, or the calculated murder of entire races of people? Do you see child abuse and incest? Adultery? Promiscuity? Alcoholism? What do you see?

What did sin look like before it had time to develop its full palette of options? What was different about these two human beings from just seconds before?

"Then the eyes of both of them were opened, and they realized they were naked; so they sewed fig leaves together and made coverings for themselves" (Genesis 3:7). Shame, fear, a desire to hide from one another...those were some of the first marks of sin. One human being was alienated from another.

For the first time in history, two people could not look one another in the eye. They had guarded thoughts and began to withhold themselves from one another. They each stood imprisoned in self. Partnership and the image of God that it modeled were shattered. The first universal effect of sin was complete: the breakdown of communication between human beings. That breakdown is still rampant in our species today.

Self-centeredness was the only reality left to a race cut off from God and from one another. "'Flesh,' that is, everything mortal about them [Adam and Eve], became very important...it was all they had."[11]

Man immediately felt cut off from God. Instead of running to greet Him, they hid. God cried out in the terrible silence, "Adam, where are you?" They did not answer. Shame, fear, and a desire to hide from God had replaced perfect friendship. The second universal mark of sin was complete: the breakdown of communication between creature and Creator.

In one stroke of genius, the enemy of our souls accomplished his purpose. Partnership with one another and oneness with God were destroyed. Alienated from one another and from God, the human race stepped into a new dimension of loneliness. Communication was broken.

Numerous studies have been done on people's fears. In polls, three things are usually at the top: the fear of dying and the fear of snakes often compete for second and third place. But the number one fear is that of giving a speech. This means most people would rather die than give a speech![12]

Isn't it interesting that the three top fears are echoes from the Garden of Eden...communication problems...a snake...death? Something so tragic, so traumatic, so fundamentally violating happened to us in the Garden of Eden that its memory still haunts our collective subconscious today.

Many of the most deeply rooted problems we have, chronic conflicts in the world, revolve around communication issues...between nations, between groups, between male and female, and between God and His creatures. To find freedom from these, we must understand our enemy and his purposes.

# Chapter Four

✷

# *Satan and Communication*

✷

*"The weapons we fight with are not the weapons
of the world. On the contrary, they have divine
power to demolish strongholds"
(II Corinthians 10:4).*

THE GREATEST TEMPTATION in my life,
and in the life of every Christian, is to not believe God.
The Bible is not so complicated to understand as it
is contrary to what appears to be true about our circumstances. For instance, even as I write this chapter, my
natural tendency is to dive in with grit and determination
and try to wrestle the thing out. I must remind myself
to pray and seek God's wisdom as I put down the words.
I have to tell myself moment by moment that my battles
are primarily spiritual.

45

Those of us who desire to follow Christ have an enemy. We're not struggling against flesh and blood, but "against the spiritual forces of evil in the heavenly realms" (Ephesians 6:12).

## The Enemy's Strategy

Satan had a specific agenda in the Garden, and he is still pushing it today. He desperately wants to destroy the image of God in mankind, and to return the human race to loneliness.

Satan does not hate human beings per se. He hates God, and he hates our capacity to manifest God's image. God is glorious, and He has made man second only to Himself in authority. Lucifer desires those positions of power and influence, and he has custom-designed a strategy to gain them. He knows that our potential to glorify God is rooted, in part, in our ability to communicate. We cannot demonstrate the love, unity, and wisdom of God to those around us if we cannot communicate.

Satan has been enormously successful at this strategy. "Emptiness and loneliness are universal afflictions...deeply experienced in every nation and across every century."[13] In one poll taken by *Psychology Today*, loneliness was the most frequently mentioned problem. Thirty-eight percent of female and forty-three percent of male readers said they often felt lonely.[14]

## The Nature of Our Enemy

C.S. Lewis said that "evil is a parasite, not an original thing."[15] Satan copies all the good things God created, then turns them upside down in rebellion. God is for truth; Satan is for deception. God wants to redeem mankind, and Satan to destroy them. God is love. Satan is filled with fury. God longs for openness and light. Satan loves secrecy and darkness. God invites us to unity and freedom. Satan divides and conquers. God's communication is based on respect for man's dignity. Satan's methods rely on lies and manipulation.

## The Spiritual Battle

We need to realize we live in "enemy-occupied territory,"[16] as C.S. Lewis said. When we step up to communicate, we are coming against someone who wants to destroy everything we do. The enemy of our souls is there to confuse both us and the ones we are trying to reach. He wants to isolate us from each other and from God. The more important our communication, the more fierce the battle.

Satan wants to destroy all our relationships by cutting the lines of communication. The greatest test we'll face in any relationship is being willing to deepen our communication level.

The day we decide to stop working at communicating is the day we begin to walk away from a relationship. If we have problems with parents, children, co-workers, fellow church members, or neighbors, we are doomed the day we decide to quit talking.

It's the same in our relationship with God. When people stop talking to God, they have begun walking away from Him. Perhaps they prayed for something and didn't get it, or had an expectation that wasn't met. The relationship starts breaking down when the silence creeps in.

The enemy wants that. He wants us to think we are so incredibly separated that we will never bridge the gap. Anything the enemy can do to cause misunderstanding among people, he will do. He whispers in our ear that the others are obstinate, belligerent, will never listen. He wants us to get our guns so loaded that when we do talk, we blast, destroying the potential for true communication. He wants us to overreact or not react at all; either will serve his purpose.

Even if we study communication skills and work on sharpening them, it will not be enough if we ignore the spiritual dimension. Our enemy's strategy must be defeated as we take back the territory of communication.

## What Are Our Weapons?

The first and last weapons of our warfare listed in Ephesians 6 are the truth—first, the truth that helps defend us (the "belt of truth"), and second, our offensive weapon, "the sword of the Spirit, which is the word of God."

To win the battle of effective communication, we must defend ourselves by believing the truth. The truth is that we can communicate, because God made us able; that He has defeated our enemy who would make us afraid even to try; that "the one who is in you is greater than the one who is in the world" (I John 4:4).

Moses told the Lord he could not communicate with the Israelite nation because he was not eloquent. God reminded Moses that He had made his tongue and could communicate through him (Exodus 4:10-11). Like Moses, we must face the fear of communication, and overcome it with the truth that God has made our mouth. We must believe Him when He says we were enriched in all speech and knowledge (I Corinthians 1:5) and when He promises to give us wisdom generously (James 1:5), and that He "will give [us] such eloquence and wisdom that none of [our] opponents will be able to resist or contradict it" (Luke 21:15 Phillips).

Our weapon of offense listed in Ephesians 6 is also the truth: "the word of God." We will make gains against the kingdom of darkness according to our knowledge of the Word of God—*the message*—and our ability to wield this sword—*the methods of communication*.

It is not enough to have the right message if we continue using the methods of the enemy. In the kingdom of God, the end never justifies the means. A righteous warrior is not only righteous in cause but in strategy. If we try to accomplish God's goals using Satan's ways, we will lose, because God must remove His blessing from us.

After listing our weapons of warfare in Ephesians chapter 6, Paul concluded by telling us to pray. This is where we wage the real war. We must fight the spiritual battle in the heavenlies before we can expect success on the ground. While we should do our best in preparation and diligence, understanding our message and God's methods, these are not enough. We must also pray!

The apostle Paul was no novice at communication. He was highly educated in two cultures, preached throughout the Roman empire, and wrote most of the

New Testament. But even Paul realized he needed people praying for him, "that whenever I open my mouth, words may be given me so that I will fearlessly make known the mystery of the gospel" (Ephesians 6:19). He couldn't fight the spiritual battles of proclaiming the Gospel without the intercession of others.

From now on, before we have a discussion, write a paper, give a speech, teach a class, or even talk to a child, a spouse, or a co-worker about a problem, let's do our homework in prayer. We must take authority in Jesus over the enemy and command him to stop trying to keep communication from getting through from God's mind to our minds, and from our minds to others'. Let's put on the mind of Christ before we put our mouths in motion (see I Corinthians 2:16 NASB).

The Lord showed me how practical this was when I faced a problem with a co-worker. I'll call her Beth. She worked with me several years in Youth With A Mission. Beth was a very needy person, so scarred at a young age that it left her requiring a lifetime of healing. If she hadn't been in a loving community, she would have probably ended up as a bag lady on the streets or in an institution. She had been around our ministry for several years, getting counseling and doing odd jobs, when she came to work in an office I managed.

Early on we agreed on a working contract: Beth was to be a responsible member of our staff, and was not to turn the office into a personal counseling clinic. She was to seek that help from appropriate people after office hours. Some days she did pretty well, other days she didn't.

One day I realized I would have to speak to Beth once again to remind her of our working agreement. But how could I give her correction without crushing her? I prayed earnestly, asking God to help me speak the truth in love.

Beth came into my office, looking awkward, as if she knew she was being called on the carpet. I offered her a cup of tea and we chatted awhile. I told her all the good things she was doing, meanwhile silently crying out to God for the way to approach this delicate confrontation.

My phone rang. When I answered it, the receptionist told me a well-known international evangelist was on the line from South Africa. I was taken aback. I was so surprised this prominent man was on the phone that I said his name out loud, with Beth sitting in front of me. Her eyes widened. Then it hit me. This was God's answer! I told the receptionist, "Tell Rev. So-and-so I am busy with an important meeting, and will get back to him as soon as I'm finished." After that, Beth was so affirmed that she was ready to accept correction without being hurt.

We can always overcome Adam and Eve's error by consulting God. This is spiritual warfare.

# Chapter Five

ംഘ

# *A Biblical View of Man*

ംഘ

*"I praise you because I am fearfully and
wonderfully made; your works are wonderful,
I know that full well" (Psalm 139:14).*

I STRUGGLED WITH THE PROBLEM for
years: I was angry at the lost. The longer I was in
Christian service, the angrier I became. Didn't these
people realize how much work it was going to take to
bring their lives around to wholeness after all that dam-
aging sin?

The trouble was that I couldn't get God to agree with
me. As I studied the Word year after year, it became
increasingly clear that Christ did not demonstrate anger
with the lost, but compassion. He said they were like
sheep without a shepherd (Matthew 9:36; Mark 6:34).

When He did express anger, it was with the "found" who were leading the lost astray (Matthew 23:27).

This was an enigma. I couldn't get my mind wrapped around it. But I realized that if God and I differed, He'd have to win. I asked Him to help me see people as He saw them.

After finishing my lectures one spring afternoon, I went walking down the streets of Amsterdam. A yellow city bus drove by with the huge picture windows typical of Dutch vehicles.

As the bus passed in front of me, its center window framed a scene that burned into my mind like a color photograph. Two figures sat beside each other on the bus: a young man with long, spiked hair colored Christmas red and a matching leather jacket, and a little old lady with the classic gray bun. Her shoulders were pushed up as though her hands might be resting on top of a basket on her lap.

The bus went by in a flash, but the image remained engraved in my mind. I felt the Holy Spirit whisper into my heart, "You see those two people as really different, don't you, Landa?"

*See them as different?* I thought. *You've got to be kidding! Of course I do.*

My immediate judgment was that the young man was probably a total rebel, up to his eyeballs in sin, while the woman was a sweet, little, old granny, just out of church, taking cookies to her grandchildren. I felt negative toward him, positive toward her.

The Holy Spirit whispered again, "I don't see any difference in them at all."

*You've got to be kidding me!* was my immediate response.

However, years of struggle and study finally brought me to the simple realization that we *are* more similar than we are different.

I believe most errors in communication—Christian and otherwise—come about because we do not understand our human similarities, and we emphasize our differences. We see rich and poor, black and white, young and old, liberal and conservative, people like me and people not at all like me.

These perceived differences become barriers to communication, telling us why we cannot reach certain people. It builds alienation. If, on the other hand, we believe we are more similar than different, we look for common ground where we can identify, tearing down the walls that separate us.

This was just one of the things I had to learn so I could see people as God sees them. Man is made the way God has made him, and we are not going to change that. It is a fixed reality. So we must understand what God has to say in the Bible about us...all of us.

## 1. We all have the same temptations.

No human being is creative enough to make up a new temptation, and no one is without these common temptations. According to I Corinthians 10:13, "No temptation has seized you except what is common to man." Each of us has seconded Adam's choice, and has engaged in sin and rebellion against God's truth. Some of us have done this by disobeying revealed truth, and others by ignoring the truth revealed to their conscience (Romans 2:12-16; 3:23). Later in this book, we will look at this topic and its implications more carefully, but for now, let's realize that it is just one of the ways we are more alike than we are different.

## 2. We all have felt needs.

Our second common trait is that we all experience *felt needs*. A felt need is an area of our life where we are aware of a lack, and are open to being helped. People may worry about their marriage, their children, crime in the streets, disease, nuclear warfare, getting better grades, or the state of the environment. The list is endless.

The great thing about the Gospel is that it relates to all of life, and we can communicate at whatever point a person is open. In chapter 11, we'll see how Jesus did it.

## 3. We are all made in the image of God.

This is the most basic fact about every human who has ever lived. Different colors, shapes, languages, genders, vocations, beliefs, geographic locations, cultures, and periods of history are only superficial. In fact, Jesus says these things have no lasting importance, for they are not found in eternity (Matthew 22:30; Galatians 3:28).

Every person ever conceived and brought into this world was made in the image of God, and that image is identical for everyone! There aren't different images of God. There is just one, and we all have it. Whether you are talking with a stone-age tribesman in the rain forest or a computer scientist working on laser beam projections in space, you are dealing with two people with the identical image of God.

The world questions what makes a human "human." Scientists have suggested it is our intelligence. Others focus on man's opposable thumbs and his use of tools as his distinction in the animal kingdom.

Still others say it is our ability to communicate, but now we have discovered that some animals—like dolphins—are quite intelligent. Dian Fossey observed gorillas in the wild communicating through 15 different sounds.[17] Within a period of two weeks, Eugene Linden was able to teach gorillas enough sign language that they were asking for food and drink. After more training, these gorillas have a vocabulary of more than 600 words, converse through a computer terminal, form simple sentences to apologize, joke, tease, argue, insult, swear, and even to lie.[18] In addition, chimpanzees have exhibited the ability to use crude tools to accomplish tasks.[19]

Any theory isolated from the knowledge of God fails to satisfy the universal sense that we are unique. We know that what sets humans apart from the rest of creation is that we are created in the image of God.

Scripture tells about four things that make us unique. In Genesis 1:26, God declared, "Let us make man in our image." As Sailhammer said in his exposition of Genesis, "The creation of man is set apart from the previous acts of creation by a series of subtle contrasts...."[20]

The first sign of uniqueness was that when God created man, He said the more personal "Let us make..." instead of the impersonal "Let there be...."

Second, other creatures were described as beings made "according to their kinds," but man's creation was described as "in our [God's] image." So man's image was not simply of himself; he shared a likeness with his Creator.

Third, gender was not stressed when the Scripture told of the creation of other forms of life, but the narrative stressed that God created man "male and female."

Fourth, only man was given dominion in God's creation, a dominion "over all the earth, and over all the creatures...." It seems obvious that the Author of Scripture intended to portray man as a special creature set apart.

So our uniqueness lies in God's gift of His image. We all have it, and it cannot be removed or lost, though it has been tarnished by our fallen state. Therefore, no matter what the communication challenge, and no matter who our audience is, we can have amazing insight if we understand what makes up the image of God.

## What Makes Up the Image of God?

In order to understand ourselves and our audience, it is imperative that we understand the image of God. The law of the image of God working within mankind is as absolute as the law of gravity. If we violate it, we can expect certain results. If we use it, the same holds true.

It is not my purpose to do an exhaustive study of what makes up the image of God, but to give enough insight to snow how profoundly it affects the area of communication. We want to look at ten attributes we corporately manifest in God's likeness: capacities of the mind, reason, and imagination, as well as our more elusive qualities of emotion, spirit, and creativity. Probably two of the most important aspects of our image as it relates to communication are our will and our God-given sovereignty. We will look at our capacity to set goals and our ability to communicate.

## We Have Emotions.

We each have a full range of emotions because God has a full range of emotions. Cultural mores and personality type may modify the way we show these emotions, but we all have them. If you are trying to be emotionless, you are not trying to be like God. God weeps (Jeremiah 48:32; John 11:35). He gets angry (II Samuel 22:8). He demonstrates frustration (Jeremiah 5:1-2; Matthew 23:37). He feels compassion (Psalm 103:13). He rejoices with singing (Zephaniah 3:17). He knows the feeling of delight (Zephaniah 3:17; II Samuel 22:20). The whole spectrum of feelings are shown in the Scripture's description of the Trinity.

## All of Us Are Creative.

I taught art in elementary school right after graduating from college. Some of my students' assignments were to make elephants from clay, and to design stained glass windows with tissue paper. I was amazed by the things they produced. Each project was unique, and somehow reflected the child who had created it. They couldn't avoid producing a work that looked like them.

All human beings are creative. It is part of the image of the Creator.

If you asked a group of four-year-old children how many could draw an elephant, most would raise their hands. If you asked a group of college graduates the same thing, probably none would raise his hand. They've decided they're not artists and can't produce a decent picture of an elephant. As we grow up, we're taught that creativity is the inheritance of the gifted few, but a child knows better.

I have watched creative North Africans fix an ancient bus in the middle of the desert, using little more than chewing gum and a rubber band. Some of us had creative moms who could produce a decent dinner out of what appeared to be "nothing" in the fridge—a handful of spinach leaves, some leftover macaroni, a can of soup. People express their creativity in every arena. We can't get away from it.

The creative capacity longs to be expressed whether an individual realizes it or not. The more we are allowed to put our unique mark on a thing, the more involved we will be, the more personal ownership we will experience. Something dries up in us when there is no room for innovation and expression. This is vital information for the communicator who wants to involve his audience.

### We Are Reasonable.

One of the worst mistakes we can make is to think of the human race as a mindless lump. The best way to understand a person's behavior is to find out the reason behind it. What are the motivating factors?

If you're speaking to a drug addict, you need to realize she made certain choices for certain reasons that led her into her addiction. Or perhaps you're communicating with an atheist. I have found it useful to ask what kind of God he doesn't believe in. Atheists always have a reason, and often describe some sort of celestial delinquent wreaking havoc on the human race. I listen and then agree with them. If I thought God was like that, I wouldn't believe in Him, either.

Let me illustrate how important it is to understand man's reasonableness when you are trying to communicate. Imagine you meet a young man in his early thirties. He is handsome, employed, and has a good car and a nice family. You ask if he has any interest in spiritual things.

He responds warmly, "Why, yes, I'm a Mormon."

You shout, "You're kidding, man! That's a cult! You gotta get out of that! You need to become a Christian!"

Now let me tell you more about this good-looking young man. Five years before, he was lying in his own vomit in the gutter, totally strung out on drugs. He had lost his job, hadn't slept in a bed in months, and didn't even know where his family was.

Two guys on bicycles wearing white shirts and black ties stopped and told him there was a better way to live. They took him home, cleaned him up, got him into a rehabilitation program, found him a job and a place to live, and even located his family for him.

Now are you going to say he's crazy for being involved in a cult? If you know the reason behind the involvement, you can approach the situation with wisdom. "Hey, I know God is thrilled with your progress. I can see why your belief is so important to you. Are there areas in your life where you're still searching?"

Nobody does anything for no reason at all! Find out the reason *before* you start communicating.

The Bible makes it clear that Jesus first loved us where we were. To a fallen race in a fallen world, sin seems like a reasonable response to life's problems. If you don't know God and His comfort, getting drunk to numb the pain is the most reasonable response after losing a close relationship. Or you may try meaningless one-night stands, substituting sex for companionship and understanding.

We should never be surprised by what people do without Him. Understanding the reasons behind what they do and what they believe will help us know how to move them toward truth. Ignoring their reasons not only closes down their receptivity to our message, but denigrates the image of God in them.

### We Set Goals.

God sets goals. He says, "Tomorrow I'm going to do this," and "Before I wrap it all up, I'm going to do that." God looks into the future and projects His actions.

Because we are made in the image of God, we set goals, too. Some people set short-range goals, and others set long-range goals. Some goals are subconscious or unarticulated, but we all have this capacity...an incredible capacity.

Did you know that the area of earth we call Los Angeles is a desert? Originally it had only enough water to sustain life for a handful of people. But our species wanted to live there even though it was uninhabitable. So the goal was set, the plans were made, and they finally figured out how to get water...from the Colorado River and eventually from much of western America!

We set goals. We look ahead in time, decide what we want, and move toward it.

Understanding the powerful motivational tool of people's conscious and unconscious goals is a great advantage for the communicator.

## We Are Spiritual.

Whether we know or believe in God or not, we are spiritual beings.

While living in the Middle East, I often traveled in and out of the region. I used to listen to Western travelers flying out of these spiritually darkened nations. They would audibly sigh as the plane lifted off, and would say something like, "Boy, it feels better already." They had no idea what "it" was, but they were sensing the spiritual climate of that country.

My parents didn't always get along when I was growing up, but they rarely argued in front of me. That didn't keep me from knowing when they were having a bad day, though. The atmosphere of the entire house was affected.

Because of mankind's alienation from God, many people get into the occult. They cannot continue to deny their God-given spiritual capacity. Academic institutions that scoffed at the Christian faith in an invisible God now teach parapsychology and other courses in the spiritual realm. People believe in reincarnation, astral projection, and such because they somehow sense that life is longer than seventy or eighty years, and that we are more than just our physical bodies. They don't know the living God, so they explore other avenues.

The ability to communicate spiritually is from God, and is to be restored to us as He renews us. Paul, preaching to the Athenians on Mars Hill, said that each of us is to seek God to, "reach out for him and find him,...he is not far from each one of us" (Acts 17:27).

Too often we Christians treat as strange or taboo what the Bible clearly states. And the Bible makes it clear that our work as Christians is to first recognize the spiritual realm and to deal with the reality of that (see II Corinthians 10:4). God's Word shows us that spiritual communication, though diminished through the Fall, is still with us.

Have you ever walked into a room and perceived that something had been going on prior to your entering? You weren't seeing or hearing anything specific; you were receiving communication in a way other than through your five senses. You were using your God-given capacity for spiritual communication.

Scott Peck tells of a series of sophisticated experiments by Montague Ullman and Stanley Krippner, in which an awake individual repeatedly "transmitted" images to a person asleep in another room, who had the same images appear in his dreams. The validity of such happenings has been scientifically proven in terms of their probability.[21] Many of us have heard stories of identical twins who were separated by thousands of miles going into department stores and buying the same suit of clothes on the same day, or who had been separated at birth, yet after being reunited, finding they had married wives with the same first name.

How do these things happen? We don't know why,

but as Christians, we shouldn't be surprised when they do. The ability to send and receive messages through our spiritual capacity is an essential understanding to the Christian communicator. In exploring spiritual realms, our response to people shouldn't be a knee-jerk condemnation. While we should give warning about tapping into the dark side of the spiritual realm, we can use this openness to spiritual things to point our generation to truth. By being interested in the spiritual realm, they are demonstrating that they are made in the image of God.

## Memory

God in His great capacity is omniscient. He knows and remembers all things.

It is said that everything we have ever experienced is stored in our brain. What we lack is the ability to access a memory at any given time. But certain sights, sounds, and smells will trigger long-forgotten memories. Sometimes counselors are able to help bring blocked memories to the surface.

This is important information for the communicator, because we are never dealing with a "clean slate." There are no audiences waiting like a sponge just to absorb our message. Our audience has myriads of stored memories which they may or may not be aware of. These existing mind maps will either help our message get through or deny it altogether.

## Imagination

God created us with imagination, and it is a powerful tool. It can move us from our own subjective experiences to understanding things we have never experienced.

I have listened to African-Americans talk about what they experience in certain circumstances, and it's similar to what I, as a female, have felt occasionally. I know what it means to be an "invisible person." It's not that you are treated poorly, it's that you're treated as if you were not there. I can also imagine, to a degree, what it is like to be a Turkish immigrant in a German factory because I have been thrown into alien environments myself. By linking up my own experience and imagining anyone else's situation, I can understand! I can walk in their shoes. This is a wonderful tool in communication.

Also, this powerful ability to imagine allows me, like God, to bring things into existence that have never been. The imagination can be used for good or for evil. It can produce a system for planting and harvesting enough wheat to feed millions of people, or it can help child molesters find victims through a computer network.

We can use our imagination in prayer, using the eyes of faith to see what a person can become, even though he looks unredeemable to us. Using our imagination under the control of the Spirit of God, we can create with Him. This gives us powerful potential.

## We Each Have the Power of Choice.

The amazing capacity of will is one of the most important human attributes for us as communicators to understand. I know the following may seem strange to say in a book devoted to communication, but communication isn't powerful; *people* are powerful.

From Day One of a baby's existence on earth, she

exhibits her free will. Ask any parent! While the rest of the animal kingdom goes about doing what instinct and the laws of nature tell them to do, the tiny human begins to make her distinctive self known.

Much infant behavior is purely instinctive. She cries when a natural need is not met: She is hungry, wet, or has a tummyache. Unlike any other species, this human child almost immediately begins to demand things she does not need but wants, even to her own harm.

She wants to be up until all hours of the night. She wants to be held by every person who comes through the door rather than getting the quiet and rest she needs. She wants to eat things that are destructive to her health.

Ever since the time of Adam, we have been making individual choices. The will is a function of our spirit. C.S. Lewis felt that we were probably created for our spirit to rule over our bodies. He surmised that the Fall into sin robbed us of some of this great capacity. Some practices hark back to the glorious beings we must have been when God first created us.[22]

For instance, we know you can slow your heartbeat at will. You can diminish the secretion of adrenalin into your system. More and more current medical treatment is based on influencing your body's responses by force of will. We don't understand it, and many people are concerned about it. But could it be that "mind over matter" works because there are abilities diminished through the Fall that we can still choose to exercise?

Human history is full of amazing stories of will. People choose to be free. Did you wonder where all the non-communists came from when the Soviet Bloc began to deteriorate? They were there the whole time. They attended their communist schools, sat under their indoctrination, heard their broadcasts, and read their newspapers. They didn't receive a differing viewpoint through any form of mass communication, yet they refused to bow to communist dogma. They did not receive the message because they did not want to!

Individuals can show an incredible force of will. I've heard doctors tell of extremely ill people who hung on for weeks or months because they refused to die. On the other hand, people who could have easily survived died simply because they didn't have the will to live.

We speak of people with "weak wills" or with no willpower. But we must be careful not to develop a distorted, unbiblical picture of humanity. God gave us a will. Is it a lack of willpower or an incredible will *to* eat that makes a person eat until they damage their body? Is it no willpower or an unbelievably strong will that allows an intelligent man to keep killing himself by smoking?

Without God's gift of the will, we would be marvelous robots operated by a great cosmic puppeteer. There would be no capacity for love, for love must be chosen in order to be true. However, the power to love also means the power to reject love and to hate.

The will is the human race's greatest and most terrifying attribute. Our choices have true significance for good or for evil. The potential misuse of our will was the price God paid for our genuine significance as creatures. The burden we bear as truly awesome beings is the responsibility for what we choose. The communicator must realize that people aren't passive recipients of life's messages and influences, but active, inventive players.

A number of years ago, it seemed we were on the verge of using terrifying communication techniques which would override the will, such as hypnosis, subliminal communication, and brainwashing. But as we learned more, the power of the human will was underscored, not set aside. Now we know that you cannot be hypnotized if you don't want to be, and once hypnotized, you cannot be made to do anything you wouldn't consciously do.

Subliminal communication was once a hot topic. The theory held that you could flash words across a film screen fast enough that the conscious mind wouldn't be aware of it but the subconscious would respond. Research supposedly demonstrated that the message "eat popcorn" flashed repeatedly across the screen during a movie resulted in increased popcorn sales.

Some may ask why we couldn't use this as a shortcut to evangelism. We could put subliminal messages on television and movie screens—messages that flashed "become a Christian," or "accept Christ"—and we would have nationwide revival. There are two problems with this: It would violate people's God-given right to choose, and it wouldn't work.

Although subliminal communication theory is still taught as fact in secondary schools and colleges all over the world, it has been refuted. Within months of the original research, it was invalidated by the scientific community. They learned that subliminal communication merely reminded people of what they already wanted. Those who loved popcorn bought popcorn. It had no affect on those who didn't like popcorn.[23]

Brainwashing was one of the most frightening concepts to come along in the middle of the 20th century. Besides being used by repressive political regimes, it moved into a whole new arena with religious cults in the 1960s and 1970s. There was serious concern that by isolating followers from family and friends, putting them through long indoctrination meetings, and surrounding them with peer pressure, cults were in fact brainwashing their recruits. As a response, parents hired experts to kidnap "brainwashed" children from cults and to "deprogram" them.

All this was built on the idea that we can easily become the puppets of fanatics. But neither science nor the Bible gives this fear serious credibility.

Research has shown that brainwashing is possible only under very limited conditions: through rare, powerful drugs which alter the brain's chemistry, or by isolating an individual from any decision-making process for extended periods of time while controlling all sensory input.[24] Outside of these extreme circumstances, a person can withstand the most vile torture and deprivation, and refuse to bow to his captors.

We are fearfully and wonderfully made in the image of God. God has a will and sovereignty, and His sovereignty is unlimited. God has given us a will and sovereignty in our own affairs. He will not intrude lightly. He respects this ability because it makes us truly creatures made in His image. If we are to communicate with others, we must honor the biblical view of man in all its aspects. We must stand in awe of every person created in the image of God.

# Chapter Six

❧

# *What Is Communication?*

❧

*"When anyone hears the message about the king-
dom and does not understand it, the evil one
comes and snatches away what was sown
in his heart" (Matthew 13:19).*

IT WAS THE SUMMER OF 1988, and the
Olympics were being held in Seoul, Korea. The event
boasted the largest international television audience in
the history of the world. This was Korea's first post-war
opportunity to show off their modern development.
Heady stuff!

East and West are light years away from each other
culturally, and nowhere was this more evident than in
what I refer to as the "bad boxing" incident. A Korean
boxer was disturbed with the way a Korean referee was

71

making calls during his televised Olympics match. So he sat down in the middle of the ring, refusing to fight.

The Korean official in the ring knew tens of thousands of people were watching live in the stadium, and millions via television around the world. He walked out and bowed politely to the boxer, Korean fashion. He spoke quietly into the boxer's ear, then returned to his corner. The boxer stayed frozen to the mat. This happened several times, with increasing numbers of Korean officials going out each time to persuade the stubborn boxer to get up.

American television producers thought this was great drama. There was no way they were going to switch to another event! This was a bizarre, funny, gutsy news story. Their cameras stayed glued to the ring. Koreans, on the other hand, were mortified. They were losing face in front of their Olympic guests and the entire world.

Finally, after lengthy negotiations, the stadium lights were turned off, and the stubborn sportsman was carried out in darkness. End of story? Unfortunately, no.

The American broadcasters chose this footage to repeat every hour on the hour. They used a clip of the defiant boxer sitting in the middle of the ring as their introduction for each commercial break. The Korean embarrassment was compounded scores of times each day during the entire Olympic Games.

The Americans thought the boxer's behavior was humorous, a bit of rugged individualism, a brave protest. The Koreans felt it was cowardly, demeaning, and humiliating. The Americans thought they were giving the public great entertainment. The Koreans felt they were being held up to ridicule.

Then an enterprising American had a great idea. He printed T-shirts celebrating the notorious boxer, and sold them on the streets of Seoul.

In order to understand the slogan he used on the shirt, you need to know that in American slang of 1988, the word *bad* meant "cool," a positive connotation. So the shirt read, "KOREA—BAD BOXING" in bold letters.

This "business genius" thought he was complimenting the Koreans, but the Koreans did not read it that way. Friends of mine who were in Seoul at that time said that for awhile it looked as if the entire American Olympic delegation might be sent home! It was a classic case of miscommunication.

## What Is Communication, Anyway?

The Webster's dictionary definition is "to convey knowledge of or information about: to make known. To reveal by clear signs. To cause to pass from one to another."[25] Dr. James Engel defines it this way: "Most authorities agree that communication takes place when a message has been transmitted and the intended point is grasped by another."[26]

The goal of communication is to convey meaningful content from one person to another. Sending the message is only half the battle. The message must be received and understood.

I constantly face a mound of correspondence. I often think about how to respond to a letter while I am doing other things. Sometimes I plan my response so much that I think I have already written and sent the letter. The problem is, no one received anything!

Effective communication is sending and receiving. Miscommunication can take place in two ways:

1. When my intended audience has understood a message different from the one I am sending, that is miscommunication. An example is the "bad boxing" story. The Americans were sending one message, but the Koreans were receiving another.

I was standing outside church one very warm Sunday morning and a teenage friend walked up to me and said, "You look hot."

I said, "No, I feel pretty comfortable."

When she looked at me with bewilderment, I realized I had just revealed my age. She meant "hot" (1990s) as in "rad" (1980s) as in "groovy" (1970s) as in "cool" (1960s) as in "nice." (When did teenagers ever say that?) We had miscommunicated.

2. The second way miscommunication can take place, according to Dr. Engel, is when my intended message is received by someone other than my intended audience.

Imagine that a married couple is celebrating their 10th wedding anniversary. They're going out with two other couples for dinner at a fine restaurant. Later they will be alone for a more romantic celebration.

During the elegant dinner, the couple exchanges loving glances across the table in the candlelight. Those silent messages say, "I love you. I'm glad you're mine." During the dessert, the adoring wife slips off her shoe and teasingly runs her toe up and down her husband's leg. But this message of affection is strangely ignored.

Her husband doesn't notice, continuing to talk to the friend next to him. Then she glances at the man sitting on the other side of her husband. His face is bright red, he is sputtering and reaching for his glass of water. Great message; wrong audience!

Miscommunication is "right message, wrong audience" or "wrong message, right audience." Many of the world's problems are based in miscommunication. Often it is not that we have been understood and disagreed with, but that we have not been understood at all.

## Hearing Words Is Not Communication.

In order for communication to take place, meaning must be conveyed. Jesus was struggling to get meaning across to His disciples. He said, "Be on your guard against the yeast of the Pharisees and the Sadducees" (Matthew 16:6).

Think about what was going on in this scene. They had just come from the miraculous feeding of more than 4,000 people. They were out in the countryside for three days, so intent on Jesus' teaching that no one had eaten. Jesus noticed this, and told His guys to do something about it. Imagine the disciples' consternation! Do something! Out here? With what?

You know the rest of the story. They found a lunch of seven loaves of bread and a few small fish, Jesus divided it, and they gave out bread and fish to 4,000 men, plus women and children. They ended up with seven baskets of leftovers.

Wouldn't you expect this experience with Jesus' miracle bread to leave an indelible mark on the disciples?

Fast forward to verse 5 of Matthew 16. The disciples were crossing the lake with Jesus, and discovered no one had brought any bread. It could have been the same day. If so, they had left seven basketfuls of bread sitting on the shore. We don't know. However, we do know that these twelve men had seen the thirteenth man in that boat feed thousands from nearly nothing.

Can't you see the scene in that boat? Someone mentioned they hadn't remembered to bring the bread.

"You did what? Seven baskets sitting there and you didn't bring one?"

Then Jesus said, "Be on your guard against the yeast of the Pharisees and Sadducees."

If we had been in the boat, we would have known exactly what He meant, wouldn't we? Not really. And the disciples didn't know, either. They decided He said it because they didn't bring any bread. It must be a "bread" warning.

Jesus broke into their discussion about bread with, "You of little faith, why are you talking among yourselves about not having bread?"

Can't you hear their mental gears turning? "Why are we talking about bread? Because that's the topic of conversation here. We just found out Pea Brain over there forgot to bring any of those seven baskets of bread!"

Jesus continued, "Do you still not understand?"

Obviously not. They were hearing His words, but they were not getting His meaning. So Jesus started giving them clues. He asked if they remembered the five loaves and the 5,000 people who were fed, and all the leftovers. Did they remember the seven loaves and the 4,000 fed, and all the leftovers? Sure, they remembered all of that. That's why they were irritated with Diphead here, who didn't even bring one loaf!

At this point, if the disciples went out and tried to preach the "word" they'd heard from the very mouth of Christ, the message would probably be, "Do not buy bread from stores owned by Pharisees and Sadducees!"

However, Jesus didn't give up until the light began to dawn for His disciples. "How is it you don't understand that I was not talking to you about bread?"

There he goes again. What is this discussion about? Like a master teacher, Jesus didn't give them answers. He gave them clues and made them think about it. Then He repeated the warning, "Be on your guard against the yeast of the Pharisees and Sadducees."

Finally, *ta-da!* They got it. "*Then* they understood that He was not telling them to guard against the yeast used in bread, but against the teaching of the Pharisees and Sadducees" (italics added).

Jesus was struggling for them to get the meaning of His words. Until they had that, they had nothing. Let's take this a step further.

## Repetition Is Not Communication.

The Pharisees of Jesus' day were deeply committed to the Word of God. They read it aloud, wore portions of it tied to themselves, memorized it, and committed themselves to its adherence in detail. They were even committed to world evangelism.

Yet Jesus leveled the most severe criticism at the

Pharisees. He didn't criticize them for their goals; He criticized them for their methods. The Pharisees quoted God's Word, but Jesus explained its meaning in the common language of the people. He drew illustrations from their day-to-day existence.

Communication is not merely hearing or repeating words. Communication is meaning. It is not the words I use, but the understanding my listener receives. If I don't successfully convey my meaning, I have failed to communicate.

In Isaiah 55:11, God declared, "So is my word that goes out from my mouth: It will not return to me empty, but will accomplish what I desire and achieve the purpose for which I sent it."

This text is often used to say that the quoting of Scripture alone is enough to accomplish God's communication mandate to reach the world. Some would take that idea so far as to say that we should not change a word or we would be tampering with "the Word" of God.

But the Word you and I are quoting is already using different "words" than the original manuscripts. We read an English translation of the Hebrew and Greek. Faithful scholars have already gone through the hard work of making it more understandable for you and me.

If repetition of the Word alone would accomplish the task, evangelism could be reduced to playing Scripture recordings on all the street corners of the world. Wouldn't that be great? The technology would be cheap, the work force minimal. Why aren't we doing that? Because it wouldn't work.

Let's try to see this in a little different light. What if you were to meet a man on the street and he said something that sounded like "Elabena mauri lan hihiea allegbegbe. Eyey wo so via akongo so saavo. Bena amesike la ho edjise la, maaku o gake aakoa agbemaya."

Then in English he said, "Well? What do you say? Come on, this is an important message. You need to respond. You don't understand? No problem. Let me repeat it a little more slowly." Then he said, "Ela...bena ...mauri...lan...hi...hiea...alleg...begbe. Eyey...wo...so... via...akongo...so...saavo. Bena...amesike...la...ho...edjise ...la, maaku...o...gake...aakoa...agbe...maya."

He asked you again, "Now is that better? No? You still don't understand?"

How many times would you let him repeat that before you walked away? Five? Ten? Two? Your patience threshold may be high, but however long you could last, you would not understand any more about the Word of God. Yet he was quoting Scripture to you. That was John 3:16 in the Ewe dialect of Togo, West Africa. Yet it couldn't accomplish anything in your life, no matter how many times it was repeated.

Then what will we do with this passage regarding the Word of God not returning void? If we follow Jesus' example, we must focus on the meaning. So the *Word of the Lord* is to be differentiated from the *words* of the Lord. The disciples in that boat with Jesus got the *words* but failed to get the *Word of the Lord* until they understood His meaning.

You have probably had the experience of reading the Bible, then later in the day being hard-pressed to remember anything you read. Words. You were reading words. But you have also probably read a Scripture text, or heard someone speak on a Scripture portion, and all of a sudden the Holy Spirit opened your eyes and you understood what that text meant. You never forget those moments. They change your life. They force you to make decisions on the basis of what you understand. The words become *the Word*. When meaning is conveyed and you understand what is said, it accomplishes what God has intended.

## The Danger of Meaningless Repetition

Jesus speaks of the futility of "vain repetitions" in prayer in Matthew 6:7 (KJV). The idea behind the constant repetitions of sounds, words, and phrases is that something repeated over and over has power. Jesus said this kind of mysticism or magic was paganism, or what the heathen did.

We can develop the same mentality in our communication. A perfectly good message can be destroyed by constant repetition.

Is the world hardened to the Christian message, or are they simply bored to death by hundreds of years of repetition? We did not learn vain repetition from Jesus. We learned it from the Pharisees.

We are all familiar with the phrase Jesus used with Nicodemus, that you must be born again. In some circles it has become the only way to express the need to be converted. We have "born-again Christians," "born-again experiences," and "born-again churches." We ask people if they have been born again.

When a President of the United States used this phrase during a television interview, describing his Christian faith, there was a proliferation of "born-again" everything—from born-again military strategies to born-again economic prospects, from born-again stock markets to born-again Hollywood careers.

Christians found this use of their term offensive. But repetition of a phrase, biblical though it may be, is not synonymous with meaningful communication. The vast majority of the President's listeners did not have a clue what he was talking about when he referred to being born again.

I have often wondered why we select phases such as "born again" as so significant over other phrases Jesus used in one-on-one encounters, such as with Zacchaeus or with the woman at the well. Why don't we have "I'm coming to your house for dinner" churches or "Can I have a drink of water?" experiences? While the experience of salvation is basic to Jesus' entire message, we only know of one time that He used the phrase "born again."

Jesus used these phrases because they had particular meaning to the people He was speaking to at that moment. If we are not careful, we can drift toward the idea of "magic language"—the idea that words and phrases have power in and of themselves, and need not convey meaning to the listener. We can become like the godless, who treat people as things, turning the most intimate and personal message in history—the Bible—into platitudes and meaningless repetition.

## Communication Is Not Technology

As we saw in chapter 1, the proliferation of communications technology can give us the impression that great communication is going on. Many Christian ministries dream of owning a television station, a radio station, or better yet, a satellite. These are wonderful tools that God can put in our hands to do His work, but there is no substitute for content. If you communicate poorly, television cameras will just allow you to communicate poorly to more people.

I was talking with the dean of one of America's Christian universities. Of all their colleges, their communications training was the most established, particularly in television. So I was quite surprised when he said their communications training had been the most difficult area. I asked him why. Surely their communications college was their strongest.

He said that was the problem. They had been so involved in providing their students with the most advanced television training available that they had produced terrific cameramen, editors, sound technicians, and directors, yet few who could communicate the Christian message effectively.

## Jesus Focused on Reaching People

Do you know why Jesus rebuked the bread-less disciples in that boat (Matthew 16:5-12)? Remember that Jesus drew their attention back to the two miraculous meals He had already served to more than 9,000 people. They struggled with the meaning of His words, "Be on your guard against the leaven of the Pharisees and the Sadducees." They missed the meaning of His actions, too. They couldn't apply the meaning of those miracles to their own lives.

Those twelve men who loved Jesus had eyes but could not see what Jesus was doing, and ears but could not hear what Jesus meant. So here they were in the boat with the very Man who had created bread for thousands from a few loaves, and they were worried about...bread.

Jesus didn't give up until they got understanding. And He has called us to do the same. We must do more than send messages; we must work with people until they understand.

This is hard work. Anyone can memorize and quote Scripture verses. Even Satan has memorized them. You have to struggle with the Word of God until you know what it means. You have to apply it practically in your own life. When the meaning of Christ's words and actions are alive to you, then you can give that understanding away. Jesus made the Gospel so simple anybody could understand it. That's our challenge: to do what Jesus did. Let's examine some of Jesus' words and deeds as a communicator in the remainder of this book.

# Part II

How We Communicate:
The Jesus Method

*"For I did not speak of my own accord,
but the Father who sent me commanded me
what to say and how to say it" (John 12:49).*

# Chapter Seven

✂∞✂

# *The Harvest Is Ripe*

✂∞✂

*"I tell you, open your eyes and look at the fields!*
*They are ripe for harvest" (John 4:35).*

I SANK GRATEFULLY into the comfortable leather seat. What a break! The airlines had bumped me up to business class, and I certainly wasn't going to argue with them. The long flight from California to Asia would be tiring enough.

I kicked off my shoes and unfolded a fresh copy of *The Los Angeles Times.*

I sat bolt upright! A headline on the first page of the second section screamed at me. It was about us...our mission...and there was my name, along with the name of the project I had been working on day and night for the past several weeks. I quickly scanned the article, my

heart sinking with every line. It wasn't good. An irra-
tional fear hit me...what if the stewardess knew my name
and said it aloud? Suddenly the business section of the
plane seemed very small.

This was only the most recent derogatory media
account we had survived over the past months. Our
mission had purchased the last of a string of flophouses
in San Pedro's Skid Row area. The others had been
bulldozed long ago, leaving empty lots as testimony of
the Los Angeles port's seedy history. This particular
hotel had weathered the storm of urban renewal primarily because of the public relations problems associated
with clearing out 20 residents who lived there in various
degrees of squalor. The Health Department wanted it
condemned. The Fire Department wanted it closed. But
no one wanted the hassle of dealing with these long-term
occupants.

My organization stepped in where others dared not
tread because we thought we could give more personal
attention to relocating these social castoffs. Besides, the
mercy/aid ministry we represented would bring a favor-
able influence to the community. Then it happened.

One of the residents, living illegally in the hotel
basement with her children without bathroom or
kitchen facilities, called the press. A barrage of headlines
followed. One read, "Elderly In Hotel Evicted By Program For Needy!"

We got calls from Indian Affairs in Washington,
D.C., inquiring about civil liberties. The Post Office
called to check on an accusation of mail tampering. The
Fire Department pulled an inspection—they were

apologetic, but had to follow through whenever anyone lodged a complaint.

We ended up in court fighting a restraining order against construction on the building. It was a nightmare!

Within a few weeks of reading that headline on the plane, the furor finally subsided. We were able to move in. Some of those residents even continued to camp in parts of the building. Nevertheless, we were able to show them some Christian compassion.

As I look back on this episode and all those messy headlines, I have to smile. This wasn't a story of how the godless media always persecutes Christian organizations. It was a story of how I had not been sensitive to apply the lessons the Lord had already been teaching me in the areas of Jesus' style of communication. I promised myself that if I were ever forced into another time of handling the secular press, I'd remember how Jesus handled communication challenges.

## A Different Approach to Communication

Jesus made a blanket statement to His disciples regarding the readiness of their audience. He said they should open their eyes and "look at the fields! They are ripe for harvest" (John 4:35). He said that even people they considered to be far from God were ready to perceive truth.

What's the most difficult audience you can imagine carrying the Gospel to? Shi'ite Muslims? Members of New York City's cultural elite? Leaders of radical gay rights groups? Seen-it-all members of the news media? Inner-city gangs? Jesus says they're ripe and waiting.

The audience is ready!

We carry around perceptions of people or groups as hard to reach, but Jesus' challenge was unqualified. "Open your eyes...They are ripe for harvest." We need to see our communication tasks from God's perspective. They may be difficult, but they are not impossible.

We must learn more than the message Jesus gave us. We must understand the method He demonstrated for carrying His message.

Jesus is our master model. He demonstrated basic principles of communication throughout His time on earth. We're going to look at how Jesus reached people, especially in His encounters with the rich young ruler, the woman at the well, and Zacchaeus.

Jesus' method was based on a complete understanding of how the human race was created. His method works because it is true to human nature.

As we study how to identify with our audience—seeking to serve them, provoking them to involvement, and working with them where they are in process—we will realize there is a cost to effective communication. The cost of Jesus' style of communication is personal humility and a willingness to lay down our lives. There are no cheap shortcuts.

# Chapter Eight

❧

# *Jesus Identified With His Audience*

❧

*"The Samaritan woman said to him, 'You are a Jew and I am a Samaritan woman. How can you ask me for a drink?' (For Jews do not associate with Samaritans)" (John 4:9).*

SHE WAS THE MC from hell.

I was nervous enough about how my audience would react to me as a speaker. It was a professional seminar for Singapore's Military Communications Department, and attendance was required, eating up the better part of their Saturday. I knew the people who had come to hear me speak on cross-cultural communications included Muslims, Shintoists, Hindus, animists, a few Christians, and a few probably classified as "nothings."

The MC stood to introduce me. "I'm glad you are all here today. Of course, you didn't have a choice if you wanted to keep your jobs." (The smallest smattering of laughter.)

"Landa Cope is our speaker. She is Dean of the College of Communication at the University of the Nations in Kona, Hawaii. Now, Dean Cope is *a Christian* and *a missionary*. But I think she will have something to say to us anyway. I hope you will listen."

The MC sat down. I could almost hear the "thud" of mental doors closing all over the auditorium. Her introduction had alienated me from most of the people there. I was now the speaker from outer space.

Conjuring up my pre-Christian concept of "missionary," I shuddered. Out-of-date, out-of-fashion, small wire-rimmed glasses, no makeup, orthopedic shoes, gray outfit with a white collar, and hair in a bun. This living gothic would pull out a huge leather-bound book and proceed for hours to tell me, in a squeaky voice, of things that had nothing to do with my life on Planet Earth.

I stood up and looked out over the sea of blank faces. If I didn't win their interest in the first few minutes the day was lost. I'd have to speak and they'd have to sit there, but no one would learn anything.

At least my wardrobe choices that morning had been inspired—not a gray suit, but a bright turquoise dress with an even brighter fuchsia jacket. My haircut wasn't great, but praise God, it was modern. I scanned the room, looked them straight in the eye, and smiled.

"I don't know about you, but my previous ideas of a

'missionary' were pretty grim," I said. (Another sprinkling of laughter.) "I saw them as really out of touch with
the way things are." (A little more laughter.)

I went on to describe my former ideas about the
"missionary type," and with each characteristic I named,
the laughter increased. The doors were opening again. I
was describing their mental picture. We had the same
negative reaction to the word *missionary.*

I continued into my lecture, breathing a sigh of relief.
I had overcome the barriers between myself and my
audience by identifying with them. They could see now
that we shared common ideas and concepts. They were
ready to hear my message.

## The Importance of the Incarnation

We often refer to the Cross as being central to our
faith. This is true, but when we isolate the Cross, we lose
its context and the greater understanding of the salvation
Christ won for us there.

Four points of Christ's life are essential to understanding what God was doing in sending His Son: the
Incarnation, the Cross, the Resurrection, and the Ascension. Each of these events reveals crucial elements of
God's strategy, but without the Incarnation, the other
three are meaningless.

The Cross won the legal right for us to be forgiven
of our sin and reunited with a holy Father (Romans
5:10-11; Colossians 1:20-22; Ephesians 2:14-18). If our
salvation stopped there, however, we would be alive in
the Spirit but doomed to the death of a decaying body
(Romans 7:24).

The resurrection of Christ's body from the tomb assures us of the resurrection of our own bodies, and our eventually becoming Christ-like (Romans 8:23; 6:5; Colossians 1:27; Titus 2:11-14). Even so, without the Ascension we might imagine ourselves like so many of literature's ghosts, wandering the universe with no place to go. It was in Christ's Ascension that He promised a place for us, an eternal home (John 14:2).

As wonderful as each of these facts are, they are all impossible without the Incarnation of Christ—God becoming human. It is this miraculous reality that begins the whole process of our redemption and teaches us how to live until the redemption of our bodies takes place. It is this part of the "great salvation" that empowers us while still living on earth (Philippians 3:21; II Corinthians 13:4).

## Who Really Stole Christmas?

We complain of the commercialization of Christmas. Many blame retailers for secularizing the celebration. What we need to see is that secularization, like darkness, is not the presence of something; it is the absence of something. If the understanding of Christmas is lost, it is because the Church has lost its revelation of the day's significance. We need a restored understanding of the meaning of God's fabulous Incarnation. The angels, the shepherds, the inn, the manger, and the three wise men are nice...but what does it all mean?

Nearly 2,000 years ago, brothers and sisters in Christ were asking these questions. According to Hebrews chapter 1, post-Ascension Christians misunderstood the Incarnation. They thought Jesus was something like an angel. The writer of Hebrews made it very clear that Jesus was superior to the angels before His Incarnation, but took a position below them while He was a man on earth.

What's so important about this? Unless we can get a gut-level revelation of everything the Incarnation means, we'll never understand our great salvation. We'll open ourselves up for major disillusionment. Hebrews 2:1 says we will drift from our faith. In addition, we'll never reach our audience.

The problem is, many are seeking a salvation that Jesus isn't offering, one without trouble or trial. They don't see that Jesus was made lower than the angels, therefore they have unrealistic expectations. They're trying to be angels, while continually stumbling and failing on earth.

Our salvation isn't unrealistic. Let's go carefully through the second chapter of Hebrews to unravel the mystery of the great salvation (2:3).

## The Great Salvation

*"This salvation, which was first announced by the Lord, was confirmed to us by those who heard him. God also testified to it by signs, wonders and various miracles, gifts of the Holy Spirit distributed according to his will"* (Hebrews 2:3-4).

Notice that the list of gifts of the Holy Spirit is an aside. They are the example, not the subject. Supernatural gifts are not the goal; they are merely signposts to direct us to Jesus.

*"It is not to angels that he has subjected the world
to come, about which we are speaking. But there
is a place where someone has testified: 'What is
man that you are mindful of him, or the son of
man that you care for him?'"* (Hebrews 2:5-6).

What a great question: "What is man that God is
mindful of him?" I often look at my pitiful humanity and
wonder why the God of all creation considers me at all.
I look at the human race and all the terror and destruction we have brought into the world, and I am amazed
at the great mercy of God in not wiping us all out.

*"'You made [Jesus] a little lower than the angels;
you crowned him with glory and honor and put
everything under his feet.' In putting everything
under him, God left nothing that is not
subject to Him."* (Hebrews 2:7-8).

This is what I call a "hallelujah" verse. We like this
one. We put it on Christian greeting cards and station-
ery. It's a promise-box Scripture, one of the 365 good
ones we like to read regularly. But look at the next
sentence....

*Yet at present we do not see everything
subject to him.* (Hebrews 2:8).

Uh oh! Back to reality.

When we look at the terrible things happening
around us on a daily basis, we know Jesus isn't exerting
His control over everything yet. And even worse, when
we look in the mirror, we know we have a long way to
go. If you knew you were going to die and live forever
just like you are today, would you be thrilled? No! Even

though you and I love Jesus and are committed to Him, everything is not yet subject to Him in our lives.

The gift of God is not "eternal-ness." Everyone is going to live forever. The gift of God is eternal "life," summed up in Christlikeness. When we see Him, we will be like Him, because we will finally see Him as He is (I Corinthians 13:12; I John 3:2).

So we hope in the future, but we live in the great "yet," the present.

*"But we see Jesus..." (Hebrews 2:9).*

Here is the point of the text. This is the anchor that will stop our drifting. Seeing Jesus....

*"...Who was made a little lower than the angels, now crowned with glory and honor because he suffered death, so that by the grace of God he might taste death for everyone" (Hebrews 2:9).*

It's important to see Jesus in His glory before and after the Incarnation, because that is our future inheritance. But it is crucial to understand what it was like for Jesus in between, while He lived on earth, because that is where we live now.

*"In bringing many sons to glory, it was fitting that God, for whom and through whom everything exists, should make the author of their salvation perfect through suffering" (Hebrews 2:10).*

Wait a minute here! If something is "being made perfect," from what state is it being made perfect? It is perfected from imperfection. This passage says Jesus was made perfect through the process of suffering. Jesus was, therefore...imperfect.

"Heresy!" we all scream. It can't be! Wasn't Jesus without sin? Right. Jesus never once sinned in His whole life. The Bible makes that abundantly clear (Hebrews 4:15). Therefore, sin and imperfection are not the same thing.

The writer of Hebrews goes on to say that both Jesus and His followers are of the same family (Hebrews 2:11). Now it's becoming clear: The discussion here is about our humanity—being part of the family of man—*not* about sinless perfection. "...So Jesus is not ashamed to call [us] brothers" (Hebrews 2:11).

What is our first response to our imperfections...our humanity? We are ashamed!

### He Is Not Ashamed of Us.

We may be dissatisfied with our progress, but Jesus isn't. He's not saying, "Boy, am I getting tired of waiting for you to get there!" He is not ashamed of our imperfections, our humanity. These words in Hebrews weren't written for some obscure spiritual problems the Jews had in ancient Rome. This text was written for us as we try to love and obey God right now. It's written to show what we can expect of life, and what it was like for Jesus.

> *"Since the children have flesh and blood, he too shared in their humanity..." (Hebrews 2:14).*

If you and I were going to be contained in mortal flesh, then Jesus would come and live out life in a human body, too. He would deal with limited energy, strength, and knowledge just like you and me.

Some may question that Jesus had limited knowledge on earth, but I believe He did. How else do we explain His prayer in the Garden of Gethsemane? "If it be your will, let this cup pass from me." He dealt with limitations so that we could overcome.

I would love to have unlimited energy, not need food, and be able to stay up night after night praying till dawn! I could be "Super Christian," leaping tall buildings in a single bound, rescuing the endangered with supernatural strength. But Jesus modeled a more humble salvation. He became tired, hungry, and distressed (Mark 11:12; Acts 10:10; Luke 12:50; John 4:6). He was God incarnate, yet He was living in a mortal body. He did all this....

*"...So that by his death he might destroy him who holds the power of death—that is, the devil—and free those who all their lives were held in slavery by their fear of death" (Hebrews 2:14-15).*

What is our fear of death? We are all going to die. Jesus didn't set us free from mortality. So what is this "fear of death" that Jesus set us free from?

The fear of death that drives the human race is the fear that they'll never be what they know they were meant to be. There will never be time to live up to the potential they know they have inside. It is the heart cry of a lost generation: "I know I look like a jerk. I know I'm trash walking around. But there's something inside of me that could be wonderful!" Death squeezes that cry to a whimpering impossibility.

Christ became human to show us that death has no

power, and that we have nothing to fear. Yes, we are mortal. We will die. But when we see Him, we will fully inherit all we were created to be (I John 3:2). We will reach His goal for us, regardless of what imperfections we might be manifesting today.

*"For surely it is not angels he helps, but Abraham's descendants" (Hebrews 2:16).*

I love this passage. It is so simple and real. So many of us are trying to be angels. I don't mean the word *angels* as those heavenly messengers who serve God. I mean, we're trying to be "angels"...nice people who are perfect all the time! The writer of Hebrews says, "Forget it! You're not an angel, and if you were you'd get no help from Jesus."

We're descendants of Abraham. Remember him? He was the guy who wanted to obey God, and ended up wandering around (Hebrews 11:8-9). If you'd met Abraham in the wilderness and asked where he was going, he'd have said, "I don't know. I'm just trying to obey God."

There are those who will try to proclaim a "better salvation." This is the real heresy. The idea that Christians can be angels—that we can be perfect—will lead to failure and sin.

A television evangelist caught in a terrible sex scandal was asked why he had done it. "I have asked myself that 10,000 times through 10,000 tears. Maybe [I've] tried to live [my] entire life as though [I] was not human."[27]

The curse of trying to appear perfect removes us from the help of Jesus, and leaves us vulnerable to sin.

This television evangelist tried to live a life that was better than Jesus—a life with no admitted temptation and, therefore, no help in overcoming temptation.

> *"For this reason he had to be made like his brothers in every way, in order that he might become a merciful and faithful high priest in service to God, and that he might make atonement for the sins of the people" (Hebrews 2:17).*

Jesus had to become like us; it was the only way to get the job done. He would have been more comfortable if He had come in all His splendor and glory, but it was not the way to reach a lost and dying world. Unlike the man who stood in the temple and prayed, "God, I thank you that I am not like all other men," (Luke 18:11), Jesus made the opposite claim. He identified wholly with us.

Isn't it interesting that Jesus only needed to come at one time in history, to one culture, to one religious background, and to one social status in order to identify with the entire human race? It didn't even matter that He came as a male and not a female. Why? Because in our spiritual essence, we are more alike than different.

If you are identifying less and less with the human race, you are getting further and further from Christlikeness. If your goal is to become more angelic, you are passing Him in the sky. Rather than exhibiting the power of the Incarnation, you are becoming useless to the cause of Christ.

> *"Because he himself suffered when he was tempted, he is able to help those who are being tempted" (Hebrews 2:18).*

Here is the key. In the next chapter, we will look in greater depth at the subject of Jesus' temptation. But because He went through the daily trial of our humanity, He is able to help us.

# Chapter Nine

⌘

# *Jesus Could Identify Because He Was Tempted*

⌘

*"For we do not have a high priest who is unable to sympathize with our weaknesses, but we have one who has been tempted in every way, just as we are—yet was without sin" (Hebrews 4:15).*

JESUS DECLARED SOMETHING for all the world to know about Himself, something which many of us who are supposedly wanting to be like Him are trying to hide. "He...suffered when he was tempted" (Hebrews 2:18).

Perhaps you have heard of some terrible crime and exclaimed, "I just don't understand how someone could do such a thing!" We aren't being honest if we say that.

The Bible says there is no temptation but what is *common* to us all (I Corinthians 10:13).

The biblical teaching on temptation is a sharp, double-edged sword: We may find we aren't as good as we thought we were, or we may realize we aren't the unique scum of the earth that we thought. We can't come up with a new temptation. And we can't experience one that Jesus Himself has not experienced and dealt with personally. He'll never say to us, "I just don't understand how you could be tempted to do that."

Hebrews 4:15 says, "We do not have a high priest who is unable to sympathize with our weaknesses, but we have one who has been tempted in every way, just as we are—yet was without sin."

Why was Jesus able to be tempted and the Father not? James 1:13 says that the Father cannot be tempted, yet Scripture makes it very clear Jesus was tempted in every way. Why? Because the Father does not have a body, but Jesus did. A human body. He bore our sin. He wore this fallen flesh of ours for 33 years, and in this human form resides every weakness and temptation known to the human race.

We can't be better than Jesus. That means you and I will have to deal with temptation every week, every day, and every hour. Remember Hebrews chapter 2 which said if we didn't understand the great salvation we would drift? Who drifts? It is the person who wants a salvation where one morning he wakes up "perfect," never acknowledging his temptation and never accepting the help of his fellow Christians and his Lord.

## Intolerance

It is so hard for us to acknowledge the truth of the Bible when it says there is no temptation that is not common to us all. But I believe intolerance is a by-product of denying our own weaknesses. Whatever type of person we find incomprehensible represents some area in our own life where we've never been tested.

"How could anyone discipline a child abusively?" you might ask. Maybe you have never been around active children for lengthy periods of time! The miracle is that not everyone overreacts toward hyperactive children.

"How could anyone murder another human being?" The root of violence is within every one of us. You may never be tempted to blow someone away with a gun, but what about blasting them with your words, or with the cold-blooded withdrawing of your affections?

## Do You Believe in Hate at First Sight?

Some time ago I was standing in the lobby of an Amsterdam hotel, bored, watching the parade of guests check in. A middle-aged woman made her way to the registration desk. I looked her over and decided immediately she was an American. But there was something else. *I didn't like her!*

This reaction disturbed me, and as I pondered my wicked heart, a man joined her at the desk. An Englishman, I guessed. And I didn't like him, either.

What was wrong with me? Here I was, a full-time Christian worker, commanded to love my neighbor, standing in a hotel lobby despising unknown people for no apparent reason.

Others lined up at the desk. That couple was obviously part of some group. I looked around the lobby for a clue to their identity, then I saw a poster welcoming the "International Peace Conference." That's who they were—"peaceniks." Middle-aged academic types, gathering to work for world peace.

*Poor, ludicrous, unenlightened souls...they missed the Jesus Revolution of the sixties. They're still in darkness!* I thought.

Compassion would have been an appropriate Christlike response, but I would have had a hard time even being civil to these people. What was wrong with me?

I asked the Holy Spirit to show me the roots of this spite. Then suddenly I could see what it was: *These people were just like me in my pre-conversion days.* Had Christ not become Lord of my life, I probably would be standing in that registration line. But why my instant distaste? It wasn't too hard once the Holy Spirit's light began to expose my heart. The problem was that I thought I was better than those people now; I had the truth. I was no longer a pseudo-intellectual groping around for answers. I had firsthand knowledge of absolute truth.

My pride reeked. It was time to say, "God, have mercy on me, a sinner!"

## Level Ground

Jesus could have come as an authority figure: King, Father, Commander in Chief. But He chose the level— or equal—ground of brother and friend. Whenever God makes a decision like that, we need to ask ourselves why. God chose to communicate from level ground because that was the best position. Jesus came alongside us, identifying with our humanity. Our communication must follow the same pattern.

Are we willing to suffer with our own temptations, and to identify with those who are suffering with theirs? You can't reach anyone you don't love, and you can't love those you don't identify with.

Among Christians there is a terrible trap: implied perfection. Even though you are not perfect, you should appear to be. If we admit to weakness, we won't be a "good witness." We work on looking like good Christians, avoiding even the appearance of evil, all the while afraid to admit what is really going on inside us.

This is not the great salvation we have to offer people. Our great salvation is a heavy-duty one for real people who face tough temptations every day. It's a salvation that comes at our darkest moments, when we have the worst of thoughts, when we want to say the most terrible things, when our emotions are rising up to hideous dimensions. Jesus comes right into those moments and says, "I understand your temptations. I am not ashamed of your weaknesses. I do not condemn you. I will help you."

If we accept the daily suffering of overcoming temptations as Jesus did, then the most important key to effective communication will be ours. We can comfort people with the comfort Jesus has given us.

## Temptation Is Not Sin.

Please don't misunderstand me. I am not saying we might as well sin because we're only human. Temptation and sin are not the same. Sin is when we give in to our common temptations and act on them, or even dwell on them in our minds.

I grew up in a blue-collar community and could swear with the best of them. When I became a Christian I didn't forget how to swear. In fact, I could probably swear more fluently today because my mind is clearer and I have a better memory. So why don't I? Because it doesn't glorify God, not because it never enters my mind.

I didn't forget how to lie when I was converted, either. I could make up some whoppers when I was a kid. Even now I'm tempted to lie in tight situations, because it could solve the immediate problem. So why don't I lie? Because it's destructive and it's wrong.

I am capable as a human being of any imaginable temptation. Admitting that is the first step to overcoming temptation and conquering sin.

## For the Sake of Balance

In these last two chapters I have tried to emphasize what we have in common as human beings, particularly in the area of temptation. You may wonder, what about our differences? Aren't these important for the Christian communicator to recognize?

Yes, of course there are differences. We have different cultures, personalities, talents, and abilities. There are also differences in gender, age, and genetic makeup. Many books have been written about how to identify differences in target audiences, both by Christian and non-Christian communicators.

However, we must understand that these differences are superficial and temporal. It is far more important to understand what the Bible emphasizes: We are all created in the image of God, and we all live in a fallen state.

We are not angels. We can lay down our halos, look ourselves in the mirror, and know that the more we know about that person in the mirror—good and bad—the more we will know about our fellow man. Then when we encounter a person who seems impossible to reach, we can say, "I know you. I can love you and help you, because Christ loved and helped me."

# Chapter Ten

❧

# *Jesus Came as a Servant*

❧

*"If anyone wants to be first, he must be the very last, and the servant of all" (Mark 9:35).*

WE HAVE JUST SEEN how dramatically Jesus identified with His audience. The second most dynamic aspect of His communication was His servant approach.

At some point in history the Church forgot this. We became focused on our message rather than on serving our audience. The burning question wasn't, "Where are people hurting? How can we apply the Gospel to meet those needs?" Instead it became, "Are we being faithful to Scripture? Is that the exact meaning of those words? Are we communicating in balance with the whole of the Bible?"

Instead of pouring our hearts into reaching people, our passion became defending the message. If God felt that way, John 3:16 would have read, "For God so loved the *message*, that He sent His only Son...."

Jesus didn't come to defend the message. The message of God's eternal truth is just fine, thank you. It stood before the creation of the earth, and it will stand when all heaven and earth have passed away (Matthew 24:35). It's people who are in danger! God so loved the *world*. Jesus came because He loved this crummy fallen creation and all its difficult inhabitants. His concern was for the audience, and His goal was to make the truth understandable to them.

We are not sent out to defend the message. We are sent out to win the ears of our listeners. We are to serve the audience, to demonstrate the power of the truth.

Do not misunderstand me: We are to be faithful to the message as God has revealed it. We are to properly handle Scripture and have a clear understanding of truth. That's the easy part. The hard part is the same challenge that Jesus had: making it understandable to our generation and culture.

Remember Dr. Engel's definition of communication? It takes place when my intended audience understands my intended message. That doesn't mean they will accept and embrace it, but they will have understood it well enough to make their decision. This is all God expects of us. But He does command that we accomplish this. If we fail to reach our audience so that they understand our message, we have failed. Period.

## Same Message, Different Audiences

Jesus and Paul had the same message, but two very different audiences. Jesus was sent to the Jews, to the House of Israel. Paul was given a specific call to take Christ's message to an entirely different audience—the Gentiles. If we compare and contrast what Jesus and Paul did, it will give us a model for our work as Christian communicators today.

Jesus looked like a Jew, talked like a Jew, worked like a Jew, and was pretty well indistinguishable from anyone else in the Jewish society of His day. When He taught He used references from Jewish culture and literature. He told stories that were set in a Jewish context. If we only had the four gospels, we might think that the way to evangelize was with Jewish music, costumes, dance, and stories.

But Scripture didn't leave us there. It went on to give us a second example. Paul was sent to the Gentiles, a completely different audience. They were not different in their basic essence as fallen human beings created in the image of God, but they were different in language, culture, and historical references.

Did Paul mimic Jesus' words all over the Roman empire? No. He went first to the wilderness for 14 years to learn from the Holy Spirit how to present Jesus' message to the Gentiles. It wasn't a question of altering the truth, but of altering the way the truth was communicated.

It was Paul's commitment to his audience that led to the first big controversy of the Church—the dispute over circumcision. Should the Gospel be taken to the whole world and to every culture, or should it stay tied to Jewish tradition and culture? Should the messengers of the Gospel simply repeat the words Jesus used, or should they use the process He demonstrated and translate the message to reach far different audiences?

Paul argued heatedly and powerfully for the latter. The Gospel of Christ was not to become a subset of Judaism. Instead of righteousness being communicating through the symbol of circumcision, it would be communicated by the symbol of having a circumcised heart. The message of righteousness would be the same, but the symbol would be changed for new cultures. Paul was serving his audience (Acts 15:5-11).

Eventually the other apostles understood his wisdom, and the controversy died down. Paul was doing exactly what Jesus had done. He was taking the Word of God and adapting it to a new people group. Jesus had shaken up the Pharisees by saying the truth in new, dynamic ways. Now Paul was rocking the established church of his day by doing the same thing.

We must continue this legacy of Christ, making the liberating truth understandable to every people group of our time.

## A Reluctant 20th-Century Paul

I know a young man named David who is like a 20th-century Paul. He has a heart for the lost, especially young people living on the streets.

A few years ago, David walked the streets of Amsterdam trying to reach the social castoffs hanging around the city corners by the thousands. These bikers, druggies, prostitutes, and punkers were known by their outrageously colored spiked hair, safety pins, and absolute despair.

I don't know if you have ever tried to speak to kids like this, but trying to engage them in conversation is like wringing water from a stone. Time after time David returned frustrated after hours of fruitlessly trying to reach the youth in these subcultures. He got nothing, no response except cold, blank faces. In frustration, he asked God for help.

The answer was surprising. The Lord told David he would have to find ways to be more identified with them.

As time passed, the Lord continued to impress him with the same thing. God made it clear that it wasn't just symbolic identification. He was going to have to be willing to be mistaken for one himself. Just as Jesus was called a glutton, a drunkard, and a sinner, David was going to have to be willing to be misunderstood if he wanted to reach these kids.

David gathered a small team of unlikely missionaries around him who also felt called to the punkers and their associates on the streets. The team prayed often and fervently for God to give them open doors and strategies that would touch these hearts. David had ministered on the streets for many years, but that did not prepare him for the nightlife of the clubs and hangouts where they needed to go. This kid from the groomed suburbs of Minneapolis, Minnesota, was in culture shock. It was like going out to war every night.

The team struggled in prayer with their dilemma.

Jesus encouraged them that these were the same problems He had faced personally in reaching the lost of His day. They must persist!

David and his team adopted new hairstyles and strategies, and went back out on the streets of Amsterdam. What happened in the next months surprised everyone. For the first time, the street kids began to see that having a relationship with Jesus had no connection with which direction your hair pointed. The sullen faces of stone opened up. The punkers were not only willing to talk, but they showed a deep desire for truth. Hundreds came to the Lord.

Now David's team had a new problem. What could they do with all their converts? They couldn't send them to existing churches. Their appearance would be too much for the gentle Christians! But they couldn't leave them to wander the streets, either. Their newfound faith must be nurtured. So they started a special Bible study with hundreds attending. What a sight they were! Looking like a group from outer space, they gathered for one purpose...to learn about Jesus.

Making contacts at rock concerts, David was struck by the influence these bands had on the audience. He realized that he and his friends needed to start a band. They began with a children's drum set, old guitars, innertube guitar straps, and no musical background. They needed a name. Someone who'd heard what they were doing said, "That sound is no longer music." And they had it. They would be called "No Longer Music."

The strategy was so simple. David was distinctly impressed by the Holy Spirit that these young people needed their own type of music to express themselves and their search.

No Longer Music became an important part of the continuing street evangelism, but the band also became an important part of the new converts' worship. They were eager to express their love and commitment to Christ...when they understood the medium.

As I write this I am reminded of the "Jesus Freaks" of the late 1960s and early 1970s. Young people were saved by the hundreds of thousands around the world in what came to be known as the Jesus Revolution. Evangelists who looked just like the hippies they were called to had to start new fellowships to hold all the young radicals coming to Christ. Besides, lots of churches had no use for the long-haired, beaded disciples in torn jeans.

Eventually Christian contemporary music was born, and Christian bookstores were revolutionized as a new generation of believers brought their flavor into the Church.

I am reminded of still another radical era, and a young innovator who dared to put Christian lyrics to beer-hall songs. The established church was scandalized, but we still sing those hymns of Martin Luther today.

### Self-expression vs. Reaching the Audience

Jesus wasn't committed to one system or one method of communication. He was committed to reaching people. Sometimes He preached in the synagogue; other times He used the forum of street debate so loved by the Jews of His day. On still other occasions, His evangelism took place in social settings, over a meal, or while attending a wedding. He used what was most effective for each person or group. His giftings weren't paramount to Him; serving His audience was.

When we debate the merits of different strategies such as door-to-door witnessing, street drama, mass rallies, one-on-one sharing, or television, we are missing the point. We are approaching a form as if it alone holds the key to communication. To unlock the heart of the audience, we must use the right form of communication...and no one form will be right every time.

## Entertaining Ourselves

Our university bought a radio station in Hilo, Hawaii, from the Billy Graham Evangelistic Association. Until that organization had pioneered the station, Hilo had been the largest community in the United States without Christian radio.

Our potential listening audience in Hilo was quite a challenge for our young team. The community was 80% Japanese and rural. They prized their isolation from faster moving communities in Hawaii. Most Hilo residents were what we call in Hawaii "local," and they were proud of it. In contrast, most of our station's staff members were Caucasian, from the Mainland U.S., and under 25 years of age.

Some of our first program meetings were quite interesting. The original format of the station was not the style of our twenty-something staff. In their estimation, there was too much preaching and teaching, and not enough music. And the music we were playing was the "wrong" music—too mellow, too boring. Who would want to listen to that?

During those program meetings, we set down clearly defined guidelines for the types of music to be played. Yet as weeks passed, the young deejays kept drifting into the style of music they liked. When confronted, they would admit they didn't even realize they were doing it. It became an intense battle, reminding our staff to serve the audience and not just entertain themselves.

We all do this. We say, "I'm into drama," or "I love apologetics." Wonderful, but are the people you're trying to reach ready for apologetics? Do they like drama? Or you may say, "I want to write literature. That's the way to reach the lost." Fine, but can your audience read? Missionary organizations have been known to send literature into areas where the people were predominantly illiterate! Why? Because literature was their thing. They did not think about the audience. They only thought about what they wanted to do in evangelism.

The first question of communication isn't, "What should I do?" or "What should I say?" You can't answer those until you answer the most important question....

## Who Is My Audience?

Who are you trying to reach? Who specifically is your audience? As Christian communicators, we often think of "the world" as our audience. "The world" is the audience of the whole Body of Christ, but which segment of that group are you or your group specifically trying to reach?

Remember the MC from hell who introduced me to the seminar in Singapore? If that had been a missionary conference instead of a multi-religious military grouping, it wouldn't have been so bad. It wasn't what my friend said; it was who she said it to.

In our communication, we need to use a "rifle" approach rather than a "shotgun" approach. A rifle releases a single, powerful bullet, and is highly accurate, even at a distance. A shotgun releases a large number of small pellets as a group, and since the power is dissipated among all the pellets, you must be very close to your target for any reliable degree of accuracy. Before we determine *what* or *how* we will communicate, we must determine *who* we are trying to reach.

When Jesus used the analogy of being born again, he was not speaking to a thirteen-year-old who had spent the last decade of his life trying to grow up. How depressing that would have been for a teenager!

Instead, Jesus used that analogy with Nicodemus, an old man who had everything life could offer except the one passion of his heart: the Messiah! Is it possible that the one fear consuming this Sanhedrin official was that he would die before "The One" came? Nicodemus risked everything to seek out Jesus, even though his brethren had already decided Jesus was of the devil. Nicodemus made it clear that he already believed Jesus' teaching and miracles were of God. The one unspoken question could only be, "Who are You?"

To Nicodemus, for whom old age threatened to snuff out a lifelong search, Jesus said, "This is not the end of your life, but the beginning....You must be born again." Jesus knew who Nicodemus was, and He served him with the message he needed.

Jesus did not use the born-again approach with others, such as the rich young ruler, the woman at the well, or Zacchaeus. He was talking to different people with different needs. He adapted His message to serve His audience.

Scripture tells us that Jesus always taught in parables when He was in public (Matthew 13:34; Mark 4:34). In the temple He used Scripture and worked from a text (Mark 12:35). The difference wasn't in the truth He presented, but in the way He presented that truth. His audience in the temple was entirely Jewish, and they believed in the authority of Scripture. The other audience was a random collection of people on the streets, both believers and non-believers. He knew who His listeners were, and He knew what they were ready to hear.

## How Does My Audience Perceive Me?

This is another important question for the communicator. We all have preconceived ideas about each other. They may be right or wrong, but they are real, and they filter all communication.

Like most daughters, I react to the simplest statement made by my mother. Someone else could say the same exact thing and get no rise at all from me. I react because she is my mother; that gives me a different interpretation of her words.

Christians have certain perceptions of non-Christians. In turn, non-Christians have certain perceptions of Christians. Westerners have perceptions of Easterners, and vice versa. These perceptions, while they may be inaccurate, are walls we have to hurdle before we can communicate effectively.

## An Unlikely Vessel

As I mentioned, street preaching is not my favorite thing. My experience, however, is that God does not always ask you to do what you like to do. So, I was street preaching in Margarra, Italy, a suburb of Venice. My audience? Three to five hundred young radicals who hung out each evening after 8:00 p.m. in the square below the Communist headquarters.

The time of evening was significant because in Italy, proper young people were not on the street after 8:00 p.m. This bunch was made up of bikers, druggies, Communists, dabblers in the occult, prostitutes, pimps, and just about any other anti-establishment type you could think of.

Before I preached the first time, I had to get over my perceptions about them. I assumed they'd be difficult—if not impossible—to reach. They were probably resistant to truth and antagonistic to the Gospel. Of course the Bible says that all things are possible with God (Matthew 19:26), and that the Holy Spirit is working to bring everyone to Himself (John 1:9; 3:19; 15:26; 16:7-9; Romans 2:15). I needed to see God's perspective of them.

But what about their view of me? Here I was, a middle-aged, middle-class, white American woman. Boring. Yawn. There was no way I could change who I was, so I had to help my audience get over their preconceived ideas of me before they could hear my message.

I spent quite a bit of time struggling in prayer over my message. It was clear: My normal communication methods would never work with this bunch. But God gave me a strategy.

When I climbed up on my box to speak that first night (yes, we used boxes to stand on), it seemed like the crowd was daring me to get their attention. Smoking, sneering, laughing, making obscene gestures...their body language screamed, "We're tough, we're cool, and we're *not* interested."

I spoke clearly and slowly: "I've come here tonight to talk about power. Spiritual power!" (No change. They kept talking, smoking, and looking anywhere but at me.)

"You already know a great deal about spiritual power," I continued. (A little less talking now, but most faces were still turned away.)

"In fact, some of you here tonight can perform supernatural feats with spiritual power, and you know they are not tricks." (Much less talking, some heads turned my way.)

"Some of you in this audience are able to control what other people do because you have spiritual power over them. And others of you know who these people are." (Near-silence in the square. Many were facing me.)

"You know that this is real spiritual power. You know that you have it. But some of you are beginning to wonder whether you control this power or if this power controls you." (Complete silence. Every eye was on me.)

"What you may not know, and what I have come to tell you tonight, is that there are two kinds of spiritual power, and they are both real. One spiritual power will ultimately control you, as it already does some of you. The other power, and the greater of the two, is a power that will set you free. If you are interested in this second spiritual power, come talk to us."

They crowded around us afterward with questions. God had overcome the barriers, both mine and theirs. The message got through. They were listening.

When Jesus asked the Samaritan woman for a drink of water at the well, it was not just His thirst He was trying to quench (John 4:7). He understood how this woman perceived Him, how someone with His background would normally perceive her, and what would overcome those two barriers. He was at the top of the social pile; she was at the bottom. He was male, Jewish, and a rabbi; she was female, Samaritan, and immoral.

Jesus asked her, "Could I have a drink of water?" She did a double take.

*How could he possibly be speaking to me?* she thought. *What's he doing in Samaria? Nice Jewish men don't come here. And how could he ask me for water? Jews never ask Samaritans for anything, let alone something like a drink of water! He'll even have to drink from my container!*

Perhaps the only way we can understand the impact of Jesus' words on this woman is to put it into a context we would understand. Imagine going up to an AIDS patient in a hospice. He has open sores all over his face and mouth, and you ask, "Could I drink from your cup?" The attitudes toward Samaritans in Jesus' day were similar to many of today's attitudes toward AIDS patients. The Samaritans were the disgusting untouchables of their day.

Jesus knew exactly what He was doing in speaking to the woman at the well. His approach got her attention.

We have the obligation to tear down barriers so that effective communication can take place. God has told us that people are alienated from the truth, but He has called us to go to them (II Corinthians 5:20). He has demonstrated that He will do whatever is necessary to serve them, and to help them overcome their barriers. The rest is up to us.

## Even Unto the Anarchists

We talked about David earlier in this chapter—the young man God sent to the punk rockers. The story got even better. Months after David and his crew formed the band No Longer Music, he was approached by the organizers of a concert for heavy metalers and punkers. They wanted No Longer Music to perform that year.

David, surprised at the invitation, said, "But we're a Christian band!" They wanted the group anyway.

David and the group got desperate in prayer. Should they even be in such an unrighteous environment? There was also the matter of their personal safety, since violence often broke out at these gatherings.

As David prayed, he heard God quietly ask, "Do they need Me, David?" The answer was obvious. When he shared this with the rest of the band, they unanimously agreed: They had to go.

As the band went onstage to perform, chaos seemed to reign in the hall. People were being knocked over, and the band could hear chairs and bottles being broken. As usual, the group put the words of their songs on a big overhead screen so everybody knew what they were singing. When No Longer Music finished their set, David explained why they were there, that Jesus was the answer, and that we need to follow Him. This was to a crowd who had written "666" all over the team's vans in the parking lot. Incredibly, young peopld gave their hearts to the Lord that night, in spite of the taunts and jeers of their friends.

Since that night, No Longer Music has been invited to play in the most radical concerts, sharing the stage with bands called The Body Bags and The Black Hole. They've ministered to anarchists, Satanists, and brawling masses of drunk and drugged kids. They have been spit on and called indecent names, they have been in danger, and have had their lives threatened. Sound familiar?

Unthinkable doors of opportunity have been opened for No Longer Music. As they have walked in God's grace and power, one thing has consistently happened: Lost sheep have been found. Young social outcasts have been rescued from the darkness, and have been brought into the light. They've given their lives to Christ as the servant heart of Jesus has broken through...again.

# Chapter Eleven

✼

# *Jesus the Communicator Met Felt Needs*

✼

*"What good is it, my brothers, if a man claims to have faith but has no deeds? Can such faith save him? Suppose a brother or sister is without clothes and daily food. If one of you says to him, 'Go, I wish you well; keep warm and well fed,' but does nothing about his physical needs, what good is it? In the same way, faith by itself, if it is not accompanied by action, is dead"* (James 2:14-17).

IT WAS A P.R. JOB I definitely didn't want. It had been a terrible year for evangelical Christians in the United States. Immorality and unethical business dealings had brought down several well-known ministers. Reporters were having a heyday with the scandals, and Christians were becoming resentful and defensive toward the media.

In this "delightful" atmosphere, my staff in Washington, D.C., was asked to handle press relations for an upcoming national prayer gathering called "Washington for Jesus." A similar rally had been held eight years earlier, with more than 200,000 participants. But even though the standard press packets were sent out, the first event had received virtually no media coverage (despite the fact that national media coverage had been given consistently to far, far smaller groups).

If you knew nothing about America except what you saw in the media, you'd think Christians were a tiny minority in the U.S. Yet Gallup polls show that 95% of Americans profess belief in God, 40% regularly attend church and 25.9% consider themselves evangelical.[28] I believe news coverage of Christian events and concerns is skewed because, according to a poll by Lichter and Rothman, 50% of the media claim to have no religious belief at all, and only three to five percent go to church or synagogue regularly.[29]

How do you get the press—mostly non-Christian, seemingly cynical—to report on a prayer gathering...especially after a year of scandals? I couldn't imagine. But as I prayed about it, I was reminded that the harvest is ripe, and the harvest includes journalists. They were our first audience as we prepared our press packets. I had to believe they could be reached.

The Lord had already been teaching me many of the principles I have shared in this book. Now I had an opportunity to put them to the test. Could we find our common ground of identification with the secular news media? Could we be servants and minister to them? And most important, could we identify their felt need so they would be willing to listen?

## Finding the Soft Spot

Given all this, plus the scandals of the previous year, we knew these journalists were going to be very suspicious of this prayer gathering. They'd probably think it was part of the religious right's political agenda. They'd heard Christians say we have the answers for our country's problems. But after the past year, that would be the worst angle we could take in our presentation.

Our team went to prayer. "Lord, what is the truth of this event that these journalists are open to? What are their felt needs? How can we reach them as individuals, Lord?"

Every person has a point of vulnerability—a soft spot. Even though the front door to their minds appears locked, there is an open back door—if you can find it. We needed to find the soft spot in these battle-hardened American journalists.

Two ideas emerged from our prayer time: First, America had huge and apparently hopeless problems. (The media would certainly agree, although they might not agree with our solutions.) Second, we as Christians accepted responsibility for our failure to live up to our own standards.

We included these two ideas in our pre-event news release packets, and mailed them to the journalists.

## God's Principles Really Do Work.

On the day of the event, I arrived at the Washington for Jesus site at 5:45 a.m. It was still dark, the only light coming from street lamps and the illuminated dome of the U.S. Capitol. As I headed toward our press tent, I was surprised to see several television network satellite trucks already there, and I hurried over to meet them.

Every major American television network was there to broadcast live. Within a short time, our tent was jammed with more than 300 reporters representing television, radio, and print outlets.

When it was all over, Washington for Jesus had received positive coverage in every major newspaper in the United States, and on radio and television in every state.

## The Felt Need

As I studied communications theory, I found there was a name for that "soft spot." It's what Dr. James Engel refers to as the "felt need." He writes, "One of the most basic principles that emerges from the study of human behavior is that *people will not change unless they feel a need to change*" (italics added). He goes on to say that we can't get people interested in the Gospel unless we can show how it's related to what they're striving for.[30]

## Jesus Used This Strategy.

I love the story of Zacchaeus. No one in town liked him. They wanted nothing to do with this scum bucket. He was a Jew who stole money from his own people for the Romans—a tax collector. The Jews considered it high treason.

Picture the scene as Jesus walked by that day. If I were to make a movie about it, I'd cast Danny DeVito as Zacchaeus. He has played lots of short, money-grubbing little men everyone loves to hate. There's Zacchaeus, played by DeVito, up in the tree waiting for Jesus. Great comedy potential here.

Have you ever wondered why Zacchaeus was in the tree? Yes, he was a short man and couldn't see over the crowd. They weren't about to let him squeeze to the front, either. They might have to cough up tax money, but they didn't have to be nice to the likes of him.

Why didn't Zacchaeus have some of his Roman soldier buddies clear a path for him? He didn't, choosing to climb a tree instead. A grown man! The ridiculous looking even more ridiculous. Evidently, Zacchaeus didn't care about his pride. He wanted to see Jesus.

Then Jesus came along, stopped, looked up into the tree, and called Zacchaeus by name. The good townspeople couldn't believe it. "He knows this little dirtbag's name? Of all the good people in Jericho, Jesus chooses this scum to speak to?" Then Jesus uttered the unimaginable. "Zacchaeus, come down immediately. I must stay at your house today."

Zacchaeus' felt need in that hostile environment was for recognition and acceptance. This ridiculed little man was open to a message of acceptance. And that was where Jesus started. What a dinner it must have been, as Zacchaeus fully repented and settled accounts with everyone in the town (Luke 19:5-9).

## Understanding the Needs

Behavioral scientists have tried to classify basic needs that human beings experience. While never exhaustive, these lists can help us get the idea. A.H. Maslow has labeled five categories of needs:

Maslow's basic concept was that the higher order of need would not come into relevance until the lower levels of need were more or less satisfied.[31]

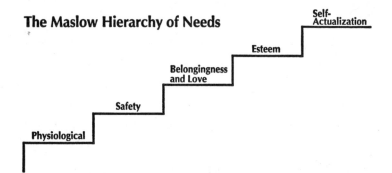

**The Maslow Hierarchy of Needs**

Physiological — Safety — Belongingness and Love — Esteem — Self-Actualization

If people's basic physiological needs—food, water, clothing, shelter—are not being met, you can't offer them anything else. If they're starving to death, the only thing you can offer that will communicate to them is food. If bombs are dropping around a refugee camp, they only want to know if Jesus has a shelter.

After physical needs are met, people have an inner desire to belong somewhere. This is what's happening in U.S. cities. Youth who grew up without fathers and with absent working mothers find a family for themselves in street gangs. They know odds are they won't live until their 21st birthday, but they have to belong somewhere.

After these more basic needs are met, the more sophisticated cries of the human heart appear. Much of the world's population never has the luxury of worrying about esteem or self-actualization. These are the felt needs of economically developed countries.

## Mr. Sony

Let's imagine that our target audience is top business executives in Japan. They are in the multimillion-dollar salary range, and let's guess that fewer than 0.5% know Christ. We need a strategy to interest them in the Gospel message. What about some traditional methods that have worked in other places.

How's this? "Mr. Sony, we have a soup kitchen down in the middle of Tokyo. Would you like to join us there for lunch?"

I don't think so.

"Mr. Sony, we have a halfway house here in the area. If you need a place to crash, just come by."

M-m-m-maybe not.

Wow, this is tough. This guy isn't open to anything.

"Uh, Mr. Sony, we have a mid-week fellowship group that gets together to study the Bible. Will you join us?"

Sorry, too busy.

"We have a testing program you can go through, Mr. Sony, to find out what your giftings are and how God has made you."

Nope.

Well, he must be unreachable. Hardhearted. Let's shake the dust off our shoes and go to those who are ready.

Wait...I have one more idea. "Mr. Sony, I know you'll agree that Japanese businessmen today need to speak English. Not only that, they need to understand the values that shape American culture, since that's your number one market. We have an English training program we can run for your top executives. We use the Bible as its text, since this will give your top people both language proficiency and culture background for their work. Interested?"

This approach has actually been used in Japan with great success.

## American Wedding, Please

Another very interesting strategy has emerged. Right now in Japan, American-style weddings are all the rage. The luckiest couples travel to the States for the wedding and at least one night of their honeymoon in an American home. Others get as close as they can to the experience right in Japan. They want all the trappings: a Christian church, a pastor, a message, the white dress, rice, wedding cake...the works.

A Japanese pastor saw the evangelistic potential in this fad, and now conducts more than 300 weddings a year. Non-Christian Japanese pay him to preach the Gospel to them! Scores have come to the Lord as Christians have met a felt need in the marketplace.

Dr. Engel points out that Christians often object to meeting felt needs, because they aren't people's real needs. Isn't this superficial?

"Much of the objection disappears when felt need is viewed as the *starting point for communication*. Few would disagree that attention must be attracted and held and that this most likely will not occur if the Gospel is presented as abstract principles"[32] (italics added).

## Jesus Understood His Audience.

Jesus used a different approach with each individual because He thought about their felt need. We've already seen how He met Zacchaeus' need for acceptance, and Nicodemus' need to meet the Messiah before he died. The woman at the well felt rejection in the form of racial and religious prejudice. Jesus met those needs and found the opening to her heart.

How hard do we work to find the felt needs of our time? What do we know about the needs of Generation X, or the homosexual community, or retirees whose children move back home? Or does the average magazine trying to sell subscriptions know a lot more about these and scores of other groups than we do?

# Chapter Twelve

❧

# *Jesus the Communicator Was Provocative*

❧

*"'Come, follow me,' Jesus said, 'and I will make you fishers of men'" (Matthew 4:19).*

MY FAVORITE KIND OF FISHING was always lake fishing with a cane pole, bobber, and a small hook with a worm. Yes, I can bait the hook myself. In fact, I love watching that brown stuff ooze out the other end. I have great childhood memories of drifting in a boat on the lake, pole in hand, drowsing away a warm afternoon. I didn't know about the right hours for catching fish. In fact, there was lots I didn't know about catching fish.

However, I did learn that fish are an independent lot.

They're in the habit of biting on their own terms. First, you have to find them. Then you have to know what and when they want to eat. Finally, you have to know the right way to wiggle the hook so they'll take a bite.

There are more sophisticated kinds of fishing than my old cane pole. Aficionados spend their entire lives and small fortunes learning the finesse of this enterprise.

Jesus took professional fishermen and said He would make them fishers of men (Matthew 4:19). He used the process of catching fish as a analogy for communicating the Gospel.

I love slapstick comedy. In several old films, the characters tried hilariously inept methods of catching fish. One guy waded into the water up to his knees, trying to catch one with his hands. Another tried clubbing them to death. That's the picture that comes to mind when I remember some of my early attempts at sharing the Gospel.

## Taking Hostages on Planes

Travel has kept me in planes a good portion of my life. It used to be that whenever I entered the cabin of an airliner I was transformed into the "great evangelical fishing machine."

*These people are going to hell, and this may be their only opportunity to receive Christ,* I thought as I buckled my seatbelt and waited for whoever was going to have to ride beside me several hours. My job was to say as much as possible about the Christian faith and Jesus in the shortest amount of time. Short hops on connector flights were the biggest challenge.

I shudder now to remember the ways I manipulated conversations to bring up the subject of Christianity. It didn't matter if they wanted to talk about Christ or not. It was my "Christian obligation" to give them the message. Oh, the scores of window seat hostages I held captive! And I had so little fruit for all my effort.

This isn't to say that the Lord can't lead us to talk to the person beside us on a plane, or wherever. But we need to be sensitive to His leading and sensitive to our audience. We need to have not only the right message, but the right method of drawing people to Him.

## Changed Thinking

Most of us have been taught that repentance is a change of direction. Before people meet Christ they're going in one direction. When they repent they "turn around" and go in the opposite direction.

What's wrong with this? It's confusing, because it sounds like we're talking about their actions changing. Haven't you met someone who doesn't even know God, yet is a much better person than any Christian you know? I've met Hindus who have more fruits of the Spirit than some of my missionary buddies! How can we say these people are lost and we are saved?

Some people don't need to change what they *do* when they repent and come to Christ. They aren't lost because of what they do or don't do, but because of what they *believe.*

A more literal translation for the Greek word for "repent" would be "changed thinking." Paul said, "Those who live according to the sinful nature have their minds set on what that nature desires; but those who live in accordance with the Spirit have *their minds set on what the Spirit desires.* The mind of sinful man is death, but *the mind controlled by the Spirit is life and peace, because the sinful mind is hostile to God*" (Romans 8:5-7, italics added)—it is unrepentant.

The lost have not changed their thinking about God. They either don't believe He exists or they don't give Him rightful place as God. The unrepentant mind does not submit to God's law because it doesn't believe in it, and it cannot please God because that mind would never ask how to obey Him (Romans 8:8).

## What Does This Mean to the Communicator?

In order to come to God, we must repent—change the thinking that is alienating us from God. In order to do that, we must be thinking in the first place! That's our job as communicators. We have to engage the minds of our listeners. We have to be provocative, getting them to ask questions. This is another major part of the communication method Jesus used.

When we realize the importance of provoking our audience to thought, we begin to understand some of Jesus' comments that make us uncomfortable. Like when He told a woman seeking healing that it wasn't right to take children's food and throw it to the dogs. Unless we understand Jesus' methods, we could have a lot of trouble with that one! Sure, He loved her and wanted to meet her need. And though this sounded like a racial slur, bigotry was totally foreign to the Son of God. He was engaging her mind so He could reach her heart. Jesus provoked questions in His audience everywhere He went.

Contrast this with most Christian communication today. How much consideration is given to what people think? Don't we emphasize what we think they need to hear instead of getting them to think and question?

## The Parable Principle

What Jesus *didn't* say is just as important as what He *did* say. Mark and Matthew each told us Jesus always used parables when teaching in public (Matthew 13:34; Mark 4:33-34). The gospel writers were emphasizing a principle of Jesus' life which we're to model today.

The parable (usually a short fictitious story that illustrates a moral attitude or a religious principle) served Jesus in three important ways.

First, storytelling is the most common and effective form of communication. In many cultures it is the way history is preserved and passed on, the way news is conveyed, and the way values are taught. Whether it is being told by the tribal storyteller around the village fire, or by Stephen Spielberg in a blockbuster movie, the appeal of a story is universal.

Second, the parable separated those in Jesus' audience who were searching for truth from those who were not (Luke 8:10). The dishonest heart missed the point of the story every time. It was Jesus' protection from those who were hostile to Him and His message. Matthew 13:10-15 shows how the parable revealed truth to the spiritual and ready mind, and at the same time concealed it from others.

Third, the parable intentionally provoked questioning, opening the mind of the listener. Jesus said, "Ask and it will be given to you; seek and you will find" (Matthew 7:7). He was always willing to give truth to sincere seekers. If they nibbled, He'd feed them a little more. But He knew their minds had to be engaged before they could make a life-changing choice. They weren't going to be manipulated into saying some magic words. He was inviting people to friendship, not capturing slaves. It had to come from within them. The parable was, "His gracious means to stimulate their thinking and awaken their spiritual perception."[33]

Isn't it sad that although Jesus welcomed questions, recognizing them as the sign of a potential disciple, we often see questions as an indication of rebellion or unbelief? Questions are the sign of an open heart and a seeking mind. Jesus loved it when people followed Him, asking, "What did You mean about the sower and the seed? What *is* the pearl of great price?" He wasn't threatened. He rewarded the questioners with more truth.

## Surprising Results

Jesus used the tool of provocative questions in His one-on-one encounters. Let's look again at the stories of the rich young ruler and the woman at the well, two classic examples with surprising results. If you don't understand the purpose of provocation in Jesus' method, these conversations appear to wander aimlessly, and some of Jesus' comments seem almost evasive. But once you see what He was up to, they become thrilling examples.

## The Perfect Prospect—The Rich Young Ruler

Don't you wish this could happen to you? You are out on the city streets, armed with your New Testament and a bunch of tracts. All of a sudden a man runs up to you, falls on his knees, and cries out, "Good teacher, what must I do to inherit eternal life?" (Luke 18:18; Mark 10:17).

Most of us would think, *Hot dog! I got a big fish on the line!*

But as we watch this scene unfold with Jesus, we're in for a surprise. Rather than whipping out the sinner's prayer and writing down the man's name and address for follow up, Jesus coolly asked the young man a question.

"Why do you call Me good? No one is good—except God alone."

To understand Jesus' question, it's important to know a little about non-Western communication. In Jesus' time and now, people from most non-Western cultures avoid asking direct questions. They ask indirect questions, considering that to be more polite. Their meaning is implied rather than stated plainly.

So Jesus was actually asking the rich young ruler, "Do you think I am God? Are you kneeling to Me because you believe I am the Messiah?"

Jesus then gave the young man the standard Old Testament answer to his question about eternal life: Keep the commandments.

In the young ruler's response we find the indirect answer to Jesus' indirect question: "Teacher...."

What word had he dropped? *Good.* Why did he stop

calling Jesus "good"? Because he was correcting himself. In the phrasing of his initial question, he had implied that Jesus was God, and he hadn't intended to. Bingo! Jesus got what He was after. When the young man rephrased his question, Jesus knew that the young man wasn't looking for the Messiah.

"All these I have kept since I was a boy," the man continued. What a religious young man! He was a religious young man who didn't know who he was talking to, a zealous young man who was on his knees in the street in front of a man he didn't even know because he was so eager for more religion. It says that "Jesus looked at him and loved him."

Jesus' next line is often misinterpreted because we don't understand what He was doing. "One thing you lack," He responded. Then because He went on to instruct the young man to sell everything, we draw the conclusion that the "one thing" he lacked was poverty. This makes nonsense out of the Gospel. Being poor doesn't give you eternal life. If it did, Calcutta would be the most righteous city on earth.

What is the one thing needed by a Jewish believer who keeps the commandments but wants to find eternal life? The Messiah! The one thing he lacked was the recognition of who Jesus was.

So Jesus provoked him a little more. "Go, sell everything you have and give to the poor, and you will have treasure in heaven. Then come, follow me." Now, what possible question do you suppose Jesus was trying to get the young man to ask? He wanted the young man to ask, "Who are you? Why should I sell everything to follow you?" But he didn't ask. He didn't seek. He didn't knock. He was looking for something else.

"At this the man's face fell." You bet it did! He had just been offered an empty field for a high cost, and he didn't see the pearl of great price in it. "He went away sad, because he had great wealth."

But Jesus put a bug in his ear designed to buzz around and around for a long time to come. "Who was that guy anyway? Why would I sell everything I own to follow him?" He was provoked.

Jesus let him walk away. Would we? I can see us running after him, calling, "Wait! You didn't understand what I meant. Let me explain a little more. Here, take this booklet with you. Let me pray for you!" But Jesus let him walk away. Why? Wasn't He interested in the young man's soul? Yes, He loved him. But Jesus understood how the Father had made His creatures. Our openness to listen is just as important as His speaking the message.

## The Worst Scenario Imaginable— the Woman at the Well

Let's contrast Jesus' encounter with the rich young ruler to His meeting with the woman at the well. In chapter 10 of this book, we saw how Jesus broke through the barriers of the Samaritan woman's perceptions of Him. Now let's look at how His conversation with the Samaritan woman, as told in John chapter 4, shows Jesus' strategy of provoking His audience.

It's hard for us to understand how disgusting Samaritans were to the Jews of Jesus' day. They felt that even the dust of Samaria would make them unholy. The very name *Samaritan* was a term of derision.[34]

So can you imagine the conversation Jesus had with His disciples when they found out where He was taking them?

"Jesus, we can't go in *there!* It's unholy. All our lives our parents and rabbis have taught us not to associate with that kind of people....Our witness could really be compromised if we're seen with that sort."

They did go through Samaria, though, and Jesus stopped at the well of Sychar, sending the others on to get lunch. As Jesus rested, a woman arrived to draw water. The time of her arrival was significant, because most women drew water in the early morning or evening hours when it was cooler. It may be that she had an urgent need for water, but her time of arrival more likely indicates that she planned her trip at a time when the other women wouldn't be around to reject her—she was an outcast in the Samaritan community.[35]

So there was Jesus, in the worst neighborhood, talking to someone even the locals looked down on. When He asked for a drink, the irony wasn't lost on her, and she took the bait, "How can you ask me for a drink? (For Jews do not associate with Samaritans.)"

In Jesus' response we see again the non-direct approach of the East. "If you knew the gift of God and who it is that asks you for a drink, you would have asked him and he would have given you living water."

She didn't swallow the bait whole. If she had, she'd have said something like, "What is this gift of life, and who are you that you could give it to me?" But she nibbled. "Sir, you have nothing to draw with and the well is deep. Where can you get this living water?"

What happened next is really surprising. This village floozy turned the discussion to history, of all things. She reminded Jesus that the Samaritans and the Jews had a common ancestor in Jacob who dug this well, and that for generations it was Jewish territory.

He wiggled the bait. "Everyone who drinks this water will be thirsty again, but whoever drinks the water I give him will never thirst. Indeed, the water I give him will become in him a spring of water welling up to eternal life."

He gave her two clues here: The Samaritan water was inadequate, and the water that He was speaking of was linked to eternal life. He still didn't make it clear what He was talking about, but alluded again to His own identity. He was subtly encouraging her to keep asking questions.

It looks like the woman began to lose interest at this point. She tossed an off-handed remark: "Sir, give me this water so I won't get thirsty and have to keep coming here to draw water."

Jesus was ready with just the right lure. "Go, call your husband and come back."

"I have no husband," she replied.

Jesus was ready again. "You are right when you say you have no husband. The fact is, you have had five husbands, and the man you now have is not your husband. What you have just said is quite true."

Jesus affirmed her for telling the truth, then demonstrated His power by telling her something He couldn't have known in the natural. He still didn't tell her who He was, though. She stayed on the hook.

"Sir, I can see that you are a prophet." She was beginning to get the idea He was someone important. Then she swam off at a sharp angle with another surprising question—a theological one. She wanted to know who had the correct form of worship, the Samaritans or the Jews.

Who would have thought this social outcast would be so interested in theology? Not only her own theology, either, but that of the neighboring country.

Jesus started to put some tension on the fishing line. He said the Jews had the right message. But, He said, a new era was here. God was doing something new, and He was looking for people who would worship Him in spirit and truth.

By this point Jesus had all but told her who He was. However, He was still being indirect, asking her in effect if she was willing to be one of those worshipers.

Amazingly, out of the mouth of this street-wise hussy came this startling declaration: "I know that Messiah is coming. When he comes, he will explain everything to us." She was looking for the Messiah. Imagine that! She was looking, and the rich young ruler—all religious and respectable—wasn't. She understood the most crucial issue of faith, and he had missed it by a mile.

Also, her statement was another indirect question, Asian-style. Jesus answered that implied question, "I who speak to you am he."

I recently went deep-sea fishing. The captain of our boat was pretty philosophical about his vocation. He said, "If you always knew for sure you were going to get one, you'd call it 'catching' instead of 'fishing.'"

Jesus went fishing for the rich young ruler. As He provoked the young man's interest, He found that the ruler was looking for the wrong things. Jesus let him walk away.

On the other hand, when Jesus began to provoke the interest of the social outcast, He saw she was looking for the Messiah. He drew her into the Kingdom.

## Finding What Is Already There

We judge from outside appearances, but God judges the inner person. We never know what is in the heart of an individual until God reveals it to us. Our job is to find however much truth they already hold within them and help them build on that. To accomplish this, we must provoke self-revelation through their own questions.

Jesus wasn't being obscure when He used unexplained parables and left comments dangling in people's minds. His words led the listener to ask questions. He was working with the human audience according to the way His Father had made them. He respected their sovereignty, never manipulating or forcing His way in. The people of His day heard the greatest communicator who ever lived, yet many still rejected the truth.

## Fearfully and Wonderfully Made

Sometimes the wonder of God's image is seen in the most extreme examples.

I have a young friend who is severely brain-damaged and autistic. He cannot speak, dress, or feed himself.

Doctors told his parents they're unsure how much he really comprehends of the world around him or the extent of his brain damage and autism.

Over the years I've been amazed to see how Jay could make himself understood without speech. Some of his adaptations were brilliant.

My young friend and I developed a certain way of wrestling. I would tickle him and poke and make fun, and in response he would reach around and twist the back of my hair and squeeze my neck with his arms as he made his version of wrestling sounds. It was a mutually understood game with a lot of physical interaction and warmth.

As we "wrestled" in the dining room one evening, a young staff member happened by. He decided to enter into our game. Uninvited, he began to tickle and tousle my friend as I had been doing. Immediately Jay dropped his head, developed a blank look, and drooled on himself. The young staffer excused himself and hurried away. As soon as he was gone, my clever friend sprang back to life, grabbed my hair, and began our game again.

We are truly fearfully and wonderfully made. Even with such limited ability to communicate, my little friend knew he deserved his integrity and sovereignty. He wasn't going to be forced to relate to someone if he didn't want to.

We must not violate the freedom God has given humans, even if our message is a godly one. We cannot make people listen. We must win their ears. We must not try to bypass their will. We must provoke them to want more, like Jesus did.

# Chapter Thirteen

❧

# *Jesus the Communicator Understood Process*

❧

*"Thus the saying 'One sows and another reaps' is true. I sent you to reap what you have not worked for. Others have done the hard work, and you have reaped the benefits of their labor" (John 4:37-38).*

SHE OBVIOUSLY HAD MONEY: I could tell by her clothes and luggage. As we both struggled toward the same train in a Swiss railway station, the handle of her suitcase broke. There are no strangers when facing the perils of travel, so I threw my bags on board and ran back to help. We had just made it up the steps when the train started moving. We found seats and sank into them.

We seemed to have an instant bond after facing that small crisis together. As she introduced herself in a very upper-class English accent, she seemed to expect me to recognize her name. I didn't. I learned that her husband was in Parliament, and was in front-page news throughout much of the world at that moment.

She asked my occupation, and finding that I had religious interest, began to tell of her amazing spiritual "journey." As the train clattered through the Swiss countryside, this woman told me all the things she had tried in her search for truth: Buddhism, Hinduism, astrology, palm reading, seances, crystal balls, voodoo. You name it and this British aristocrat had tried it!

As she told me her story, a pattern began to emerge. She had walked away from each of these experiments, taking with her some crumb she'd found helpful and rejecting the rest. I could see she was on a journey toward truth, but her path had gone through some very treacherous passages.

I listened politely, but inside my heart, a battle was raging. I didn't want to violate this woman's integrity by pouncing on her with all the Bible verses in my arsenal, but I was also afraid for her. Everything in my traditional background said, "Pluck her out of the fires of hell now! Bring her to Jesus." Yet some other part of me whispered, "Not yet. She's on the right path. Help her find the next step."

Which was the voice of the Spirit? What would Jesus have done if He had been sitting on this train?

In the midst of my turmoil she suddenly asked,

"Well, what do you think?"

What did I think? *Dear God,* I prayed silently, *don't let me fail this woman now.* I opened up to her, telling what I was feeling. I said, "You know, everything you've told me indicates you have a great love for the truth. If you continue the way you have, you will end up finding the One who is all truth, which is what I believe you're searching for. But I have to tell you, if you become dishonest with yourself, you are walking a very dangerous road."

I had her complete attention. She heard and received every word I said.

Before there was time for more, our train pulled into the station. She thanked me and was gone. I would never see her again. Had I let one slip away? I don't think so. I've weighed this conversation time and again before the Lord, and I've become convinced that I planted the seed the Spirit gave me for her. Another person would water the seed. She was in process.

## Decisions

No one wakes up one morning and says, "Oh! I have to get married today. Let's see, I'll have to meet someone. We'll need to fall in love. We'll need to book a church and invite our friends and family."

By the time two people walk down the aisle, both have made thousands of decisions over a period of time. They have weighed numerous little things about each other. "I like this; I don't like that, but I can live with it." They consider all the pros and cons: the other's appearance, personality, tastes, tone of voice, mannerisms, family, future, and finances. If you happen to live or work with someone going through this evaluation process in a relationship, he or she can drive you up the wall.

Decision-making is a process, and we take it a step at a time. Some people do it faster, some slower. But we must set the pace for ourselves. It puts us on the defensive if someone else tries to dictate that speed.

One of the important skills when communicating the Gospel is being able to recognize where people are and how to move them along in the process.

## How Jesus Did It

Jesus understood the importance of giving people the right amount of information at the right time, and of withholding information they weren't ready for.

Several times in His ministry, evil spirits cried out of people, blurting out His true identity. In Mark 1:24, a demon spoke out, "What do you want with us, Jesus of Nazareth? Have you come to destroy us? I know who you are—the Holy One of God!" Jesus immediately silenced the evil spirit.

Luke 4:41 says, "Moreover, demons came out of many people, shouting, 'You are the Son of God!' But he rebuked them and would not allow them to speak, because they knew he was the Christ."

What motivated Satan to declare the deity of Jesus? He certainly wasn't trying to recruit more disciples for Jesus. He was trying to trip Jesus up, tempting Him to give too much truth too soon. Defensive barriers would have gone up between Jesus and His audience. Jesus knew his listeners weren't that far along in the process, so He silenced the demons.

He showed His understanding of process with both the rich young ruler and the woman at the well. With the young man He held back, but He led the woman into a full conversion experience.

## Paul Understood Process.

The apostle said to one audience, "Everyone who calls on the name of the Lord will be saved" (Romans 10:13). But he said that to Orthodox Jews. They already knew who God was, understood His laws, and realized they were sinful and needed a perfect atonement. The only thing missing for this audience was accepting Jesus as the Messiah.

Compare what Paul told those Orthodox Jews to what he said to the pagans of Athens. He began with the concept of a supreme being. "I saw your many altars, and one of them had this inscription on it—'To the Unknown God.' You have been worshiping him without knowing who he is, and now I wish to tell you about him" (Acts 17:23 Living). They weren't ready to hear about Jesus and His message. They needed a basic concept of God first.

In his book *Contemporary Christian Communications,* Dr. James Engel outlines some basic steps in the decision-making process.[36]

In Dr. Engel's chart on the following page, we see the logical progression of decision-making as an individual comes to Christ. One step leads to another. Remember: Repentance is changed thinking. We have to grasp certain things before we can progress to the next step.

**The Complete Spiritual Decision Process**

| God's Role | Communicator's Role | | Man's Response |
|---|---|---|---|
| General Revelation ↓ Conviction | Proclamation | -8 | Awareness of Supreme Being |
| | | -7 | Some knowledge of Gospel |
| | | -6 | Knowledge of the fundamentals of Gospel |
| | | -5 | Grasp of personal implications of Gospel |
| | | -4 | Positive attitude toward act of becoming a Christian |
| | Call for Decision | -3 | Problem recognition and intention to act |
| | | -2 | Decision to act |
| | | -1 | Repentance and faith in Christ |
| Regeneration | | | New Creature |
| Sanctification | Follow Up | +1 | Post-decision evaluation |
| | | +2 | Incorporation into Church |
| | Cultivation | +3 | Conceptual and behavioral growth • Communion with God • Stewardship • Internal reproduction • External reproduction |
| | | • | |
| | | • | |
| | | • ↓ Eternity | |

## Manipulation vs. Measured Communication

When we consider process, some worry that this may be manipulation. Shouldn't we lay all the truth out and let people make up their minds?

We need to draw a distinction between concern for our audience and deceptive manipulation.

*Manipulation* means "to control or play upon by artful, unfair, or insidious means especially to one's own advantage."[37] It is intentional misrepresentation for the purpose of persuasion.

*Measured communication,* on the other hand, seeks to understand where listeners are, and to find the aspect of the message they are ready to consider at that point. Provoking their involvement and answering their questions allows them equal involvement in the communication process and protects their God-given sovereignty.

With measured communication, we honor our listeners' right to choose. With manipulation, the communicators attempt to bypass a person's rational choice and to entrap them.

Look again at Dr. Engel's chart on the previous page. Do you know where the vast majority of Christian communication is directed? It's concentrated on stages -3 to 0. Yet more and more of the world's population have no concept of the Gospel. They're in stages -8 to -4. We need to see where our audience is and begin communicating to them at that level.

## One Step Forward Is Successful Evangelism.

Any process that moves someone closer to the truth or even closer to an openness to the truth is successful evangelism. It's dangerous to think we have to take each person to an encounter with Christ in one conversation. This thinking builds pressure that can actually cut off communication.

I spent one summer in Paris giving out gospels of John in a cleverly devised newspaper format. I usually stood at the top of an escalator coming out of the Paris subway. Thousands of people poured up and out onto the street each hour.

After a few hours, I became quite aware of the body language people used as they saw me about to hand them a paper. Some were open to receiving it, but many tried to make their hands invisible, slumping in such a way that you couldn't put anything in their hands. They made eye contact just long enough to imply that they didn't like what I was doing, but not long enough to invite any exchange.

I know literature evangelism is effective with some people, but I wasn't sure this was the best method that day in Paris.

I liked those people. I liked them because I identified with them. Like them, the last thing I wanted in a busy schedule was something more to think about and another thing to read. I didn't want to push them further away from an interest in the Gospel.

Then I devised a plan. I'd give a gospel of John to the open ones. But my goal for those who obviously didn't want it would be to show, with a smile and a shrug, that it was okay if they didn't want the literature. I tried to let them know through my body language that there were moments when I thought this was a dumb thing to do, too. Maybe the next time they'd be more open.

I know this sounds pretty insignificant. It's not as exciting as reporting how many conversations you had with people, and how people many made decisions for Christ. Remember Jesus, though. He was willing to not talk about who He was. He was willing to let people determine how far *they* wanted to go in the process. He was willing to work with them at their level.

## The Audience Sets the Pace.

I was asked to give my testimony at a Christian Women's Club luncheon in Geneva, Switzerland. As we ate our lunch, one of the leaders discreetly pointed out a young woman at another table. "She's been coming to our meetings for the last three years, and she always writes 'atheist' on her attendance card," she said.

After giving my testimony, a number of women gathered around, asking the usual questions. Then someone behind me said, "When you were an atheist, did you have lots of questions that no one would answer?"

I turned, saw our atheist friend, and said with great enthusiasm, "Yes! Do you?" She said she did. We arranged a time to talk about her questions.

Weeks later we met in an airport restaurant several hours before my flight. She sure did have questions—she must have been saving them for years.

We talked non-stop for three hours on the deepest and most pressing issues in Christianity. After each round I'd kind of relax, thinking that would probably be enough for her to think about for awhile. Then she'd plow into the next major issue. I was exhausted.

As my flight time approached, I knew I had to bring our talk to a close. I was faced with the dilemma of what I should do, torn between my evangelical tradition and another urging.

Finally I said, "You know, I really think I have told you everything I know about the Christian faith. Do you feel you have understood it well enough to evaluate?" She felt she had.

I continued, "I'm really torn here. One part of me says, 'Pray with her now. She needs to make a decision.' Another part of me says, 'This is the most important decision she will ever make in her life. Let her take time to be sure.' I have no idea what God will require of you, but I do know that He wants complete control of your life. What do you think?"

"I really appreciate the opportunity to think about it," she replied.

"Great!" I said. "You don't need me around to help you make a decision. That's between you and God. You can transact that business with Him whenever you're ready. But I encourage you to make a decision soon, while it's fresh in your mind." I left, encouraging her to call and let me know what she decided, and praying for her to be guided by the truth.

She telephoned when I returned from my trip a couple of weeks later. I knew immediately by her tone of voice that she had decided to give her life to Christ and was a new person.

We still keep in touch 15 years after she made that decision. She has walked through some staggering waters with little support or fellowship, but that contract with God, signed on her own in full recognition of the cost, has held.

## What's the Point?

The harvest is ripe, and God has given us the tools we need to be harvesters. Whether we are talking about global evangelism or reaching our own teenager, Jesus has demonstrated for us how to reach people in a manner consistent with the way they were created. We must see people as God does, and practice the principles He does.

God loved us so much that He sent His Son to be like us, identifying with our every human condition. Jesus came, serving us where we are and provoking our longing for the truth. He moved us along in a process, and was willing and patient enough to go one step at a time. He never violated the human integrity His Father had given us when He created us. He fought the spiritual fight necessary to break through. He commanded us to go do what He had done, and encouraged us that we would accomplish these things and greater (John 14:12). I believe it!

So who is it you're trying to communicate with? Is it a loved one, a mate, a child, an obnoxious neighbor, a lost tribe, a co-worker, a castoff from society, the press, the voting constituency? You can do it. Follow the example of Christ...to the glory of God!

# Some Further Thoughts

༄

*In the process of writing this book, we may have posed questions still to be answered. I offer the following for your thoughtful consideration.*

THE AFRICAN HEAT SHIMMERED across the glaring sand as a small group gathered for the morning ceremony. A large hole had been prepared, and a long box lay at its edge. Salu was happy. His day of public declaration had come. He lay down in the box, the lid was put in place, and the village elders slowly lowered him down into the opening. The eldest intoned a prayer as each member of the small band tossed a handful of sand on top of Salu's tomb, fulfilling their part in the worship service.

As they circled the "grave," their shadows fell across their brother in the box. The elder declared, "In the name of the Father, the Son, and the Holy Spirit, I pronounce you dead to self and alive in Christ!"

Praise erupted as the lid was thrown off and Salu jumped out, a new man. He was the newest convert of the small tribal fellowship, and had just been baptized into the Kingdom.

## Different Is Not Demonic.

When we understand that communication lies in the meaning that is conveyed, not in the symbols that are used, we can develop a new way of looking at things that are different.

As we think of Salu's dry baptism, the question is what Jesus meant by the ceremony of baptism. Was that message conveyed in this desert version of baptism? And why did Jesus use water as a symbol?

Water was often used as a symbol of righteousness or purity among the Eastern peoples in Jesus' day. It is still used by both Jews and Muslims in ceremonial cleansing. When John the Baptist and Jesus chose water as the symbol of death to self and resurrection into the righteousness of God, it was already a familiar cultural symbol.

Truth is universal and eternal; symbols are not. In fact, the symbol itself can come to mean just the opposite of the intended message.

Take our African tribe, for instance. They resided in a region of desert where water is so scarce they would never use it for anything but drinking. It sustains life and is given the greatest respect. In their culture, water is never used for cleaning things or taking baths. That would be a sacrilege against the value of life.

If we were to take any of the traditional baptism ceremonies into this tribe, whether immersion or sprinkling, the message we would convey would be that life is so valueless that we can throw it away. That isn't the message of Christ's baptism. It is just the opposite: Life is so valuable that Christ died to save it. Since the message received by this tribe through a traditional baptism would be much different from what we intended, we cannot use water as an appropriate symbol of baptism in their culture.

But Salu's experience in the coffin, with the sand, has all the meaning Jesus conveyed to His audience. Dead to self! Alive in Christ! It works! The intended message is understood by the intended audience. The truth is conveyed and understood.

## Teen Mean

I heard a story of a pastor who gave his youth group permission to hold an evening youth service in the main sanctuary. In a bold stroke of trust, he gave them sole responsibility for this event, without adult supervision.

The pastor stopped by his office that night to pick up something he had forgotten. This required walking through the sanctuary. As he moved quietly up the outside aisle, he noticed that the teens were gathered in a circle at the front. Drawing nearer, the pastor was horrified to see that they were taking communion with Coca-Cola and potato chips.

He was furious. He went in his office, closed the door, and began to pray. "Lord, what a sacrilege! Please forgive them!" He alternately fumed and prayed and finally asked, "Lord, what should I do about this?" To his surprise, the Lord began to remind him of the original communion setting. Twelve men sat around a holiday table. The identical setting, food, and environment could be observed in virtually every Jewish household in that region on that night.

With the drink of the day—the one found on any ordinary table—Jesus suggested they drink in remembrance of Him and His blood. With the starch of the day—bread—He told them to remember His flesh. There were no specially made cups, no wafers with crosses on them. These were friends gathered around an ordinary festive meal of their day, and those were the symbols Jesus chose to have them remember Him.

The pastor was humbled as he realized that the teens were trying to recapture something of that original moment. When friends gather around a table these days, they often share Coca-Cola and potato chips. And what were these young people in the sanctuary doing? Remembering Christ's shed blood and broken flesh for them. Maybe they had a greater grasp of the meaning of the original ceremony than those receiving communion on Sunday morning.

## Dynamic Equivalency

There are two methods used in translation of Scripture. One is called "formal correspondence," and is basically word for word substitution. The second method of translation is called "dynamic equivalency." Here the sentence and thought are taken as a whole, and the translator attempts to find wording that will have the identical impact on the modern reader that it had on the original reader.[38]

If you apply dynamic equivalency to the personal

presentation of the Gospel, Jesus was a perfect dynamic equivalency of His Father, lived out in Jewish culture. He talked, lived, ate, and celebrated like a Jew. Why? Was it because the best way to communicate the Gospel to all people would be to use a Jewish format? No! It was because the specific audience God gave Him was the Jewish people. But Paul, a Jew, was called to reach Gentiles. After his 14 years of self-imposed exile, Paul came out preaching the Gospel in a radically different way, aimed at the Gentiles. The meaning was identical, but Paul had done what Jesus had done. He received revelation of the dynamic equivalency for the Gentile audience. We are to continue to do the same for our intended audience, as Jesus told us in John 14:12.

## Eternity in Their Hearts

In 1974 Don Richardson wrote the missions classic, *Peace Child.* The book "chronicles the agony—and the triumph—of [the] attempt to probe one of the world's most violent cultures to its foundations and then to communicate meaningfully with members of that culture."[39]

During their work with the Sawi tribe of Irian Jaya, the concept of "redemptive analogy" began to form in Richardson's thinking. Redemptive analogy—the application to local custom of spiritual truth—represented "God's keys to man's cultures" and "the New Testament-approved approach to cross-cultural evangelism."[40] They were truths sustained in the culture and tradition of the people that opened a door for them to understand the meaning of the Gospel. These are the "dynamic equivalencies" of truths in the culture.

## Two Accomplishments

Finding the "dynamic equivalence" keys accomplishes two things essential to communication and change. First, it allows intended meaning to be conveyed. Second, it allows understanding to rise up from within the person or culture, resulting in ownership.

## Conveyed Meaning

As we discussed earlier, communication is inseparable from meaning. In order for me to act on your message, I must grasp what you are trying to say. Richardson's attempts to communicate with the Sawi were frustrated each time. He was shocked when they expressed delight at Judas' betrayal. He learned that the Sawi's most revered character trait was treachery. With this approach it was impossible for them to perceive Jesus as the "good guy." Judas was the "good guy."

However, digging deeper into the cultural tradition, Richardson found the perfect way to convey to the Sawi what Christ had done for us. In this violent tribal society there was only one way to stop the revengeful killing of warring clans. One family had to give a son to the enemy family as a "peace child," a symbol of trust. Then the killing could stop. The child's new family would raise the child as their own. The most disgraceful thing a Sawi could do would be to harm the "peace child."

That was it! That was the dynamic equivalency of God's Son sent to bring "peace on earth." Jesus was God's "peace child," and we had killed Him. The light went on. The Sawi understood. Now it was a matter of their making a decision on how they would respond. The intended message had reached its intended audience.

## Truth from Within

Truth is not something that can be laid over the top of our values like a thin veneer. It rises up from within. This is why the "law was powerless" to accomplish what needed to be done for our salvation. It was an external system of rules that did not change us, but only succeeded in showing us by how much we missed the mark (Romans 8:1-4; Acts 13:39; Hebrews 7:18).

However, the Spirit working from within is able to bring true repentance or changed thinking, remaking us into the likeness of God. An authentic move of the Holy Spirit will be an expression of the truth dynamically equivalent to the host culture or person. This is the subject of another book. But the principle is so important that I want to give you enough information to provoke further thought. It is perhaps best if I illustrate what I mean.

## The African Challenge

At the current growth rate of the African church, the part of Africa south of the Sahara should be 80% Christian by the end of this century. That will make Africa the most evangelized continent in the world. But there is a fierce war being waged by the northern Islamic nations to take the territory south of them for the Muslim faith. They have finances on their side, but they also have two devastating arguments.

The first is, "What does Christianity do for the people?" What practical fruit of this Christian faith is observable? The tragic answer in many of these poor, chaotic, disease-ridden countries is, "Nothing." I believe this is the result of the Church's emphasis on salvation separated from an application of faith to everyday life.

The second argument is, "Islam is an African religion." This is simply not true. Islam is a Middle Eastern religion. The original adherents were neither black nor African. But this argument strikes at a most vulnerable spot: The Church hasn't communicated the Gospel cross-culturally.

As a whole, the African church looks Western. More than the Gospel has been transferred: It has been packaged in Western culture. And the very thing Paul fought so hard to keep from happening to the first-century Gentiles has happened to Africans. Paul fought to keep Christianity from becoming a subset of Jewish culture, because Christianity was a message for all peoples in all places, at all times. It is not to be the subset of anything, not even western culture. Paul's definition of dynamic equivalency was stated in I Corinthians 9:22: "I have become all things to all men so that by all possible means I might save some."

Africa isn't the only place where the Church can be accused of imperialism, subverting the culture of the people to a foreign belief. The Maori Christians of New Zealand have a terrible conflict in their lives: They feel they may be Christian or Maori, but not both. This is a tragic dilemma, one which God did not create. God made them Maori, and wants them to find the dynamically equivalent expression of His truth in their culture.

## Melchizedek

Don Richardson pointed out in his book *Eternity in Their Hearts* that Abraham realized Melchizedek worshiped the same God that he did. Abraham called God by the Jewish name "Yahweh," and Melchizedek used the Canaanite name "El Elyon," but comparisons of the meaning of the two names describe the same God. Abraham tithed to Melchizedek as a priest of the one true God. The truth of God had risen up within Melchizedek's culture, and they were worshiping Him in their own way.[41]

Richardson gave many examples of the power of dynamic equivalency in his books. One dramatic illustration came from early evangelism and translation work done in Korea by the Protestants and the Catholics. The early Catholic missionaries insisted on using the Chinese name for God, Shang Ti, in their translations. On the other hand, Richardson says:

> Records indicate that Protestants genuinely believed, after investigating Korean understanding of the supernatural world, that Yahweh could have only one name in Korea— *Hananim*!...The choice of Hananim could not have been more providential for Protestant missions in Korea! Preaching like houses afire in cities, towns, villages or in the countryside, Protestant missionaries began by affirming Korean belief in Hananim. Building upon this residual witness, Protestants masterfully

disarmed the Korean people's natural antipathy toward bowing before some foreign deity. Speaking directly to a public already wistfully curious about Hananim, Protestants echoed the apostle Paul's proclamation at Lystra: "In the past, [Theos] let all peoples [including Koreans] go their own way [choosing Shamanism, Confucianism or Buddhism in preference to Him]; yet he did not leave himself without witness" (see Acts 14:16-17).[42]

Our job as communicators is to find the truth residual within cultures and individuals and build on that, creating an understanding of the Gospel on the measure of truth from within.

## What About Syncretism?

Webster's defines *syncretism* as "the combination of different forms of belief or practice."[43] Dr. Engel speaks of this as a "contaminated message," blurred and uncertain because the biblical message has been indiscriminately integrated with the culture. The truth then becomes obscured.[44]

This is the opposite of what we were speaking of with dynamic equivalency. Not every cultural symbol can be used, because some do not convey the truth of the Gospel. In fact, some must be rejected, because they convey the opposite of biblical teaching.

An example of this is the Sawi tribe's reverence for treachery, which led to perpetual genocide. Wherever cultural values and God's truth disagree, culture is wrong, and must be reevaluated. However, no culture is left without a witness of truth, just as no culture is representative of all truth. Critical analysis is essential.

## What About Imperialism?

I have tried to understand what the opposite error to syncretism would be. I think I'd call it "cultural imperialism." *Imperialism* is defined as "the policy, practice, or advocacy of extending the power and dominion of a nation...."[45] This word usually refers to territory, economics, and politics. But the broadest use of the word is "the extension or imposition of power, authority or influence." Cultural imperialism takes place when one culture assumes power and authority over another.

In Christianity, cultural imperialism is present when we automatically assume that one cultural symbol of conveying the truth of the Gospel is superior to others. It makes the *symbol* the absolute truth rather than the *meaning* of the symbol. It implies that "because we sing these hymns; baptize this way; take communion this way; sit, pray, and build our places of worship like this; you should, too." The end result is that the truth is trapped in a cultural format alien to every people group other than our own. This is exactly what Paul fought against. The truth of the Gospel was not to become trapped in Jewish culture or any other culture. It was a truth for all peoples, for all time. It was a truth that was meant to find dynamic equivalencies in every tongue and tribe. God is the God of all peoples. No culture should have to see God as foreign.

A Samoan friend came to me and said, "I've had major revelation. All my Christian life, it's been hard for me to feel close to God when I pray. I couldn't figure it out, because I love God and want to be close to Him. Just this week I realized what was wrong. In Samoan culture, when you speak to someone you respect, you start by listing their past accomplishments and positions. If you were to skip this greeting, you would be showing disrespect. When the missionaries came to my island, we learned to pray the way they did. I now realize that I have never shown God respect in the way that I, a Samoan, need to."

Cultural imperialism is every bit as destructive as syncretism, and is perhaps the most dangerous deterrent to evangelism.

# Endnotes

1—David Barrett and Todd M. Johnson, *Our Globe and How to Reach It* (Birmingham, Alabama: New Hope Publishers, 1990), 25.

2—United States Center for World Mission, "The Finishable Task" chart (USCWM).

3—*The Bruskin Report* (New Brunswick, New Jersey: Bruskin Associates, 1973), 1.

4—James F. Engel, *Contemporary Christian Communications* (Nashville, Tennessee: Thomas Nelson Publishers, 1979), 47.

5—A.W. Tozer, *The Pursuit of God* (Camp Hill, Pennsylvania: Christian Publications, Inc., 1982), 73.

6—Morgan Scott Peck, *The Road Less Traveled* (New York: Simon & Schuster, 1978), 270-271.

7—Donald M. Joy, *Bonding Relationships in the Image of God* (Dallas, Texas: Word Publishing, 1985), ix.

8—*The Expositor's Bible Commentary*, Genesis, Regency Reference Library (Grand Rapids, Michigan: Zondervan Publishing House, 1990), 46.

9—*The New Brown-Driver-Briggs-Gesenius Hebrew-English Lexicon* (Peabody, Massachusetts: Hendrickson Publishers), 9.

10—Donald M. Joy, *Bonding*, 17.

11—David C. Needham, *Birthright: Christian, Do You Know Who You Are?* (Portland, Oregon: Multnomah Press, 1979), 23.

12—*The Bruskin Report*, 1.

13—Richard Wolff, *The Meaning of Loneliness* (Wheaton, Illinois: Key Publishers, 1970), 31.

14—Jeffrey Young, "Loneliness May Create Serious Health Risks," *U.S. News and World Report* (17 September 1984): 74.

15—C.S. Lewis, *Mere Christianity* (New York: Macmillan Publishing, 1952), 50.

16—C.S. Lewis, *Mere Christianity*, 51.

17—Ed. Charles Moritz, *Current Biography Yearbook* (New York: The H.W. Wilson Co., 1985), 122.

18—Francine Patterson and Eugene Linden, *The Education of Koko* (New York: Holt, Rinehart & Winston, 1981), cover and 146.

19—Christophe Boesch and Hedwige Boesch-Achermann, "Dim Forest, Bright Chimps," *Natural History* (September 1991): 53.

20—*The Expositor's Bible Commentary*, Genesis, 37.

21—Morgan Scott Peck, *The Road Less Traveled*, 253-254.

22—C.S. Lewis, *The Problem of Pain* (United Kingdom: Fontana Books, 1940), 69-71.

23—James F. Engel, *Contemporary Christian Communications*, 56.

24—James F. Engel, *Contemporary Christian Communications*, 57.

25—*Webster's Ninth New Collegiate Dictionary* (Springfield, Massachusetts: Merriam-Webster, 1987), 266.

26—James F. Engel, *Contemporary Christian Communications*, 38.

27—Michael Isikoff and Laura Sessions Stepp, "Evangelist Swaggart Steps Down," *Washington Post* (22 February 1988): 16.

28—Richard N. Ostling, "In So Many Gods We Trust," *Time* (30 January 1995): 72.

29—Robert Lichter, Linda Lichter, and Stanley Rothman, *The Media Elite: America's New Power Brokers* (Mamaroneck, New York: Hastings House, 1986).

30—James F. Engel, *Contemporary Christian Communications*, 110, 117.

31—James F. Engel, *Contemporary Christian Communications*, 112.

32—James F. Engel, *Contemporary Christian Communications*, 117.

33—*The Expositor's Bible Commentary*, 8:654.

34—*The New Compact Bible Dictionary* (Grand Rapids, Michigan: Zondervan Publishing House, 1967), 519.

35—*The Expositor's Bible Commentary*, 9:54.

36—James F. Engel, *Contemporary Christian Communications*, 225.

37—*Webster's Ninth New Collegiate Dictionary*, 724.

38—James F. Engel, *Contemporary Christian Communications*, 272.

39—Don Richardson, *Peace Child* (Glendale, California: G/L Publications, 1974), 10.

40—Don Richardson, *Peace Child*, 288.

41—Don Richardson, *Eternity in Their Hearts* (Ventura, California: Regal Books, 1981), 29-30.

42—Don Richardson, *Eternity in Their Hearts*, 68.

43—*Webster's Ninth New Collegiate Dictionary*, 1197.

44—James F. Engel, *Contemporary Christian Communications*, 24.

45—*Webster's Ninth New Collegiate Dictionary*, 604.